>PAST<

LIVING
IN THE
YESTERS

A SELF HELP BOOK ON

UNFORTUNATELY
HOW WE LIVE

[dwelling on memories]

by

ANKI JAIN

DEDICATION

To all those who have sought to break free from the shackles of the past to those who have dared to embrace their present, and to those who continue to write their stories with courage and resilience. May this journey of self-discovery inspire you to live a life brimming with purpose, joy, and freedom.

CONTENTS

PREFACE

In the tapestry of human experience, the threads of the past often hold us captive. We carry the weight of memories, both cherished and painful, and they shape our perceptions, our choices, and ultimately, our destinies. While the past has its place in our lives, it is the present moment that holds the power to truly transform us.

This book, **>PAST< Living in the Yesters**, is an invitation to embark on a journey of self-discovery. It explores the intricate relationship between our past and present, recognizing the influence of our experiences while empowering us to break free from their limitations.

Through captivating stories and insightful guidance, we'll delve into the human tendency to cling to memories, both good and bad, and uncover the profound impacts of this attachment on our well-being. We'll discover the allure of nostalgia, the weight of unresolved emotions, and the fear of change that can keep us tethered to a past we may no longer serve.

But this book isn't just about recognizing the negative impacts of dwelling in the past; it's about reclaiming the power of the present. We'll explore practical tools and strategies to cultivate mindfulness, embrace forgiveness, and rewrite our narratives. We'll learn to navigate cultural norms and personal growth, embracing the transformative power of living fully in the present.

It is my hope that this book will serve as a beacon of light, guiding you toward a more fulfilling and liberated life. As you journey through its pages, I invite you to open your heart, embrace vulnerability, and awaken to the infinite possibilities that lie within your reach.

INTRODUCTION

Have you ever found yourself caught in a loop, replaying the past in your mind? Perhaps you're haunted by a painful memory, clinging to the glory of a bygone era, or wrestling with the fear of repeating mistakes. It's a familiar human experience – the pull of the past, the weight of yesterday.

In a world that constantly demands we look forward; it can be challenging to truly let go of the past. We hold on to memories, both good and bad, believing they define who we are. Yet, the past is a river, forever flowing, and our attachment to its currents can leave us stranded in the present, unable to fully embrace the possibilities that lie ahead.

>PAST< Living in the Yesters delves into the complexities of this human experience. It recognizes the influence of our past on our present, but it also presents a powerful message of liberation: We are not bound by the past, nor defined by it. We have the power to rewrite our narratives, release the burdens of yesterday, and create a future that is brighter and more fulfilling than we ever imagined.

Throughout this book, we'll embark on a journey of self-discovery. We'll explore the intricate web of memories that shape our lives, learn to recognize the subtle ways the past can limit us, and discover the profound power of embracing the present moment. We'll uncover the roots of regret, the fear of change, and the allure of nostalgia, and we'll learn to navigate these complexities with grace and wisdom.

Through relatable stories of Indian characters, we'll examine the unique challenges of navigating cultural norms and personal growth within a society steeped in tradition. We'll see how the weight of past experiences, from societal expectations to personal failures, can shape our perceptions and influence our choices.

But this book is not just about acknowledging the past. It's about reclaiming the present. We'll discover the transformative power of mindfulness, learn the art of forgiveness, and unlock the secrets of building resilience. Through practical exercises and inspiring stories, we'll equip ourselves with the tools and strategies to navigate the complexities of life, embrace change, and create a future that is truly our own.

So, dear reader, are you ready to embark on this journey? Are you ready to release the burdens of the past and step into the liberating embrace of the present moment? I invite you to open your heart, turn the page, and let the journey begin.

1

UNDERSTANDING THE WEIGHT OF PAST

The Power of Memories

Our memories are the building blocks of who we are. They shape our identity, define our values, and influence our decisions. Each memory, whether a joyous celebration or a painful loss, carries within it a powerful message that informs our present and shapes our future. Like threads interwoven into a tapestry, our memories weave together the intricate fabric of our lives, making us who we are.

Imagine a child, newly born, a blank canvas of potential. With every experience, every interaction, every moment of laughter and tears, their memory bank starts to fill. The first touch of their mother's hand, the warmth of the sun on their face, the taste of sweet milk, these seemingly insignificant moments are etched into their minds, forming the foundation of their understanding of the world. As they grow, the tapestry of their memories becomes more intricate, woven with the threads of family traditions, childhood adventures, and schoolyard friendships.

Memories are not merely passive recordings of the past; they are active participants in our present. They shape our perceptions, influence our reactions, and guide our choices. For instance, a child who experienced a traumatic event might carry the memory of fear and distrust, affecting their interactions with others and their ability to trust in the future. Conversely, a childhood filled with love and support might cultivate a sense of security and optimism, empowering the individual to face life's challenges with resilience.

This is the power of memory: to color our world, to influence our actions, and to define our very selves. However, while memories serve as invaluable guides, they can also become chains, binding us to the past and preventing us from fully embracing the present.

The human mind has a remarkable ability to revisit past experiences, bringing them back to life with vivid detail. We can feel the rush of emotions, hear the echoes of voices, and relive the sensations of those moments, even years later. This ability to access our memory bank can be a source of comfort, allowing us to revisit cherished moments or find meaning in past experiences.

But it can also become a trap, keeping us tethered to the past, reliving painful moments, and hindering our ability to move forward. We might find ourselves dwelling on past regrets, replaying moments of failure, or longing for a past that can never be reclaimed. This constant revisiting of the past can become a source of anxiety, sadness, and frustration, preventing us from fully engaging with the present and embracing new possibilities.

The stories we tell ourselves about our past hold immense power. These narratives, shaped by our memories and the meaning we assign to them, influence our beliefs about ourselves and the world. If we cling to a past filled with negativity, we risk creating a self-fulfilling prophecy, believing that we are incapable of change, that we are destined to repeat the patterns of our past.

Consider the story of a young woman named **Priya**, who grew up in a small village in India. She dreamed of becoming a doctor, but her family insisted she focus on getting married and starting a family. Despite her aspirations, she succumbed to societal pressures and married at a young age. However, her dream of pursuing medicine never faded.

Years later, now a mother of two, Priya still felt a deep pang of longing for her unfulfilled dream. She blamed herself for giving up, for not being strong enough to stand up for her aspirations. She carried the weight of this regret, fueling a sense of disappointment and dissatisfaction with her life.

Priya's story illustrates how memories can become powerful narratives that shape our self-image and influence our actions. By constantly dwelling on her past regrets, Priya limited her ability to find fulfillment in her present life. She allowed her memories to define her identity, creating a self-narrative that was rooted in feelings of inadequacy and missed opportunities.

The challenge lies in recognizing the power of our memories, understanding how they shape us, and learning to navigate them wisely. We cannot simply erase the past, nor should we deny its impact. But we can learn to detach from the emotional grip of certain memories, to reframe our narratives, and to reclaim our present moment.

It is not about forgetting the past but about learning to process it in a way that empowers us to move forward. By understanding the weight of our memories and acknowledging the influence they have on our lives, we can begin to cultivate a healthier relationship with the past, one that allows us to embrace the present with open arms and to create a future filled with possibility.

The journey of reclaiming our present requires understanding the delicate balance between acknowledging our past and moving beyond its limitations. This journey begins with a deeper exploration of our memories, embracing their power while acknowledging their potential to hold us captive.

Think of it as navigating a vast landscape, where each memory represents a different terrain. There are mountains of joy, valleys of sorrow, and winding paths of regret. Instead of becoming lost in the labyrinth of the past, we must learn to navigate these terrains with awareness and discernment.

This journey begins with recognizing the cultural influence that shapes our relationship with memory. In many cultures, particularly in India, the past holds immense significance, influencing our values, beliefs, and even our daily rituals.

For centuries, Indian traditions have emphasized the importance of respecting elders and honoring ancestral wisdom. This reverence for the past is deeply embedded in the cultural fabric, shaping how individuals perceive their place in the world and the importance of family lineage.

However, this strong emphasis on the past can also lead to a tendency to dwell on the past, to cling to traditions that may no longer serve our present needs, and to resist change.

Imagine a young Indian woman named **Anjali**, raised in a traditional household, where family expectations weighed heavily. She was encouraged to prioritize her family's needs over her own aspirations. She was told that a woman's duty was to care for her husband and children, to maintain the household, and to uphold family traditions.

While Anjali deeply cherished her family and respected their values, she also felt a growing desire to pursue her own ambitions. She felt a yearning to explore her creative talents, to pursue a career in design, and to carve her own path in life.

But the weight of cultural expectations, the memories of past generations, and the fear of disappointing her family kept her from fully embracing her dreams. She felt torn between her desire for personal fulfillment and her sense of duty to her family.

Anjali's story is a poignant reminder of how cultural norms can shape our relationship with the past, often influencing our choices and limiting our potential. While acknowledging the importance of respecting our cultural heritage, it is crucial to find a balance between honoring traditions and pursuing our own aspirations.

The journey of reclaiming our present often involves navigating the complexities of cultural expectations and honoring our own unique journey. It requires acknowledging the influence of the past while simultaneously embracing the possibilities of the present.

In the next chapter, we will delve deeper into the specific impacts of dwelling in the past, exploring how unresolved emotions, limiting beliefs, and the fear of change can hinder our personal growth. We will also examine the allure of nostalgia, the comforting embrace of past successes, and the dangers of clinging to a past that can never be reclaimed.

By understanding the ways in which our memories shape our lives, we can begin to cultivate a healthier relationship with the past, one that allows us to embrace the present with a renewed sense of purpose and to create a future that is both fulfilling and true to ourselves.

The Cultural Tapestry

The cultural tapestry of India, woven with threads of tradition, beliefs, and values, plays a significant role in how we relate to the past. It's not just about the weight of our personal memories but also the collective history, the stories passed down through generations, and the societal expectations that define our lives. This cultural context often dictates how we view success, failure, loss, and even happiness. It shapes our understanding of what it means to live a good life, and how we should navigate our journeys.

Imagine a young woman, **Maya**, growing up in a traditional Indian family. She excels in her studies, dreams of becoming a doctor, and is driven by a desire to make a difference in the world. However, her family, deeply rooted in their cultural values, expects her to follow a more traditional path - to get married, settle down, and prioritize family over her personal ambitions. This cultural pressure creates a tension within her, pulling her between her own desires and the expectations of her family. Maya's journey is not unique; it reflects a common struggle many individuals face in navigating their own path while respecting the cultural norms ingrained in their upbringing.

Within this tapestry, the past holds a significant place. It's not just about individual memories but also the stories of ancestors, the wisdom passed down through generations, and the cultural narratives that shape our understanding of the world. We are often told stories of our ancestors, their struggles, and their triumphs. These stories instill a sense of belonging, connect us to our roots, and provide us with a framework for navigating life. They teach us about values, traditions, and expectations, shaping our understanding of what is right and wrong, what is acceptable and what is not.

The past is also deeply woven into the fabric of social norms. Cultural expectations around marriage, family, career, and even social interaction are influenced by past experiences and traditions. These expectations can be both supportive and restrictive. They can provide a sense of stability and belonging but also create pressure to conform and limit our choices.

For example, the concept of **"duty"** is deeply ingrained in many Indian cultures. We are often taught that it's our duty to take care of our parents, siblings, and extended family. This sense of duty can be a source of strength and support, but it can also lead to feelings of obligation and sacrifice, limiting our freedom to pursue our own ambitions. The past, through its influence on cultural norms, can create a sense of responsibility that can sometimes feel overwhelming, leading to a life lived for others rather than for ourselves.

It's important to recognize that cultural norms, while often valuable and enriching, can sometimes become restrictive. They can create limitations and expectations that may not align with our individual desires or aspirations. This is where the challenge lies: finding a balance between honoring the past and embracing the present. The past can provide valuable lessons and guidance, but clinging to it too tightly can prevent us from evolving and growing. The key lies in acknowledging the power of the past, understanding its influence, and then choosing to consciously create a present and future that aligns with our own values and aspirations.

This journey of personal growth and cultural navigation is not about rejecting our past but about understanding its influence, its weight, and then finding ways to move forward in a way that honors our roots while embracing the possibilities of the present. It's about embracing the beauty and richness of our cultural heritage while also recognizing that we are individuals with our own dreams, aspirations, and journeys to embark on.

The Allure of Nostalgia

The allure of nostalgia is a powerful force, a siren song that beckons us back to simpler times. It's the warmth of a childhood memory, a familiar aroma that evokes a sense of belonging, the echo of a past success that whispers promises of greatness. We hold these fragments of yesterday close, cherishing them as if they were tangible treasures, a reminder of who we were and what we once had.

This longing for the past is not inherently bad. In fact, nostalgia can be a source of comfort, a haven from the uncertainties of the present. It provides a sense of continuity, reminding us that we have lived through triumphs and survived challenges. It can be a potent antidote to the loneliness and isolation that often accompany our daily lives.

Consider the elderly gentleman, seated on his porch swing, his eyes gazing at the setting sun. He reminisces about his youth, the vibrant colors of the market, the laughter of his childhood friends, the love of his life. These memories are precious jewels, a testament to a life well-lived. They offer solace, reminding him that even in the twilight of his years, he is surrounded by a tapestry of love and joy.

However, the danger lies in allowing nostalgia to consume us. When we become fixated on the past, it can cast a shadow on our present. It can lead us to romanticize the past, overlooking its complexities and imperfections. We might begin to believe that everything was better back then, ignoring the growth we have experienced and the lessons we have learned.

The allure of nostalgia can also lead us to compare ourselves to past versions, feeling inadequate in the face of past successes. We might become fixated on achieving a "golden age," striving to recapture the feeling of our carefree youth, only to discover that the present offers its own unique joys and challenges. This relentless pursuit of a bygone era can leave us perpetually unsatisfied, yearning for a past that is forever out of reach.

Take, for instance, the young woman who struggles to find fulfillment in her current career. She reminisces about her college years, when her passions burned brightly, and her future seemed limitless. Now, burdened by the weight of responsibilities and the demands of adult life, she feels trapped in a job that doesn't ignite her soul. She clings to the memories of her former self, her dreams of becoming a writer, a musician, a free spirit. The present seems dull, overshadowed by the brilliance of her past.

It is essential to acknowledge the power of nostalgia while also understanding its limitations. While it can offer comfort and a sense of belonging, it can also become a barrier to progress. It's like a beautiful, ancient tapestry that we hold onto, but its beauty lies in its story, not in preventing us from weaving new threads of our own.

To truly live in the present, we must acknowledge the past without letting it define us. We must embrace the wisdom and lessons it offers, while also recognizing that the present holds its own unique opportunities for growth and fulfillment. The past is a part of us, a foundation upon which we build our lives, but it should not become a cage that traps us in its shadows.

Think of the past as a teacher, a wise mentor who has seen much and learned much. We can learn from its experiences, its triumphs and its setbacks, but we should never forget that our journey is not over. We are still writing our story, and the present offers a blank page, a chance to create a future filled with purpose, joy, and fulfillment.

This realization often comes through a gradual process of self-reflection and awareness. It requires us to acknowledge the power of nostalgia while also recognizing its limitations. We can find solace in the past without becoming its prisoner. It involves embracing the present, with all its imperfections, as a fertile ground for growth and fulfillment.

Let's look at some practical ways to navigate the allure of nostalgia and use it constructively:

1. Acknowledge the Past:

- Recognize that the past has shaped who you are today. It's the source of your values, your beliefs, your experiences.

- Acknowledge the good and the bad, the joys and the sorrows. Embrace it all, for it has contributed to your unique story.

- Reflect on your past without judgment. Allow yourself to feel the emotions associated with past events, but do not get lost in them.

2. Identify the Roots of Your Nostalgia:

- Ask yourself, "What am I yearning for?"

- Is it a sense of freedom, a feeling of belonging, a specific achievement?

- Understanding the underlying emotions can help you address them in the present.

3. Embrace the Present Moment:

- Engage your senses. Pay attention to the sounds, smells, tastes, textures, and sights around you.

- Practice mindfulness. Engage in activities that bring you to the present moment, such as meditation, yoga, or spending time in nature.

- Take small steps to break out of your comfort zone. Explore new hobbies, connect with new people, embrace challenges.

4. Find Fulfillment in the Present:

- Identify the things that bring you joy in the present moment. It might be spending time with loved ones, pursuing a hobby, or simply enjoying a quiet cup of tea.

- Celebrate your accomplishments, no matter how small.

- Practice gratitude for the good things in your life.

5. Cultivate a Growth Mindset:

- View challenges as opportunities for growth.

- Embrace change and learn from your mistakes.

- Remember that you are always evolving and growing, and that the present holds the potential for a brighter future.

6. Seek Support:

- Talk to a trusted friend, family member, therapist, or mentor.

- Share your experiences and seek guidance from those who understand and support you.

- Join a group or community that shares your values and interests.

Stories of Letting Go:

Throughout history, countless individuals have wrestled with the allure of nostalgia, ultimately finding the strength to move forward. Here are a few inspiring tales:

- **The Story of the Artist:** Imagine a renowned artist, their career flourishing, their name synonymous with artistic genius. However, they are haunted by the ghosts of their past. A devastating break-up, the loss of a loved one, a period of artistic drought. These past events cast a dark shadow over their present, leaving them unable to fully embrace their success. They find themselves constantly comparing their present work to their past achievements, finding fault in their every creation.

Through therapy and introspection, they learn to acknowledge the power of their past, the lessons it taught them, the resilience it fostered. They come to understand that their past experiences, while painful, have shaped their artistic vision. They realize that the present offers a new canvas, an opportunity to create art that is infused with the wisdom and experience of a life well-lived. They reclaim their passion, embracing the challenges and joys of their present journey, and begin to create a body of work that transcends their past triumphs, a testament to their enduring spirit and artistic evolution.

- **The Story of the Entrepreneur:** Picture a successful entrepreneur, their company a powerhouse in the industry. They have built a legacy, a symbol of innovation and progress. However, they are plagued by the fear of repeating past mistakes, a fear that limits their vision and inhibits their growth. The memory of a failed venture, a financial setback, a partnership that went sour - these events linger, casting a pall over their current endeavors. They hesitate to take risks, to embrace new ideas, haunted by the specter of failure.

Through self-reflection and mentorship, they learn to understand that their past experiences, while challenging, have provided valuable lessons. They acknowledge the fear, but they refuse to let it dictate their future. They embrace a growth mindset, recognizing that setbacks are inevitable, but they can also be catalysts for innovation. They learn to navigate the complexities of the present, to make calculated risks, and to seek the support of trusted advisors. They build a strong support system, a network of mentors, investors, and colleagues who encourage their growth and offer guidance. They begin to see failure not as an end, but as a steppingstone towards greater success.

The allure of nostalgia is a powerful force, but it does not have to hold us captive. By understanding its roots, embracing the present, and cultivating a growth mindset, we can navigate the past and build a future filled with purpose, joy, and fulfillment.

Recognizing the Chains

The chains of the past can be subtle, yet powerful. They bind us to a world of "what ifs" and "should haves," preventing us from fully embracing the present. Imagine a tapestry, woven with threads of memories, both bright and dark. Each thread represents an experience, a feeling, a moment etched in our minds. Some threads are vibrant, reminding us of joyous occasions, the warmth of loved ones, the thrill of achievements. Others, however, are somber, reminding us of failures, losses, and hurtful encounters.

The past, in all its complexity, shapes our perception of the present. We carry its weight, both the positive and negative, in our hearts and minds. The good memories, the triumphs, the laughter shared, these can provide comfort, a sense of nostalgia, a longing for simpler times. However, even these positive threads, when clung to too tightly, can become a barrier to our growth. They can prevent us from embracing new experiences, from reaching for new dreams, from allowing ourselves to evolve and change.

The chains of the past become especially heavy when burdened by negativity. The wounds of past failures, the scars of betrayal, the grief of loss, these are threads that can bind us to a cycle of pain. We may replay these moments in our minds, allowing the sting of hurt, the fear of repetition, to dominate our thoughts and emotions. This constant dwelling on negativity can create a sense of stagnation, a feeling of being trapped in the past, unable to move forward.

Consider the individual who experiences a significant setback in their career, a painful job loss, or a failed business venture. The memory of this experience can become a heavy weight, a constant source of anxiety. They may fear repeating this failure, avoid taking risks, and even limit their ambitions. They may harbor resentment toward those they perceive as responsible for their downfall, creating a vicious cycle of bitterness and anger. This constant replaying of the past can make it difficult to see new opportunities, to pursue new goals, to find joy in the present.

The past can also manifest in our beliefs about ourselves and the world. If we have experienced rejection, we may develop a belief that we are unworthy of love or acceptance. If we have faced financial hardship, we may develop a belief that we are destined for poverty. These limiting beliefs, often formed in the crucible of past experiences, can become ingrained, shaping our actions, our decisions, and even our self-perception. We may sabotage our own success, avoid opportunities that could bring us happiness, and live in a constant state of fear and insecurity.

The past, with its mix of positive and negative threads, holds immense power. It can provide comfort, a sense of identity, and a framework for understanding our present. However, when we allow it to dictate our present moment, to hold us captive in its grip, we lose the ability to truly live. We limit our growth, our happiness, and our potential.

Recognizing these chains, acknowledging their presence, is the first step towards liberation. It is about understanding the weight of the past, not in a spirit of self-blame or regret, but with a compassionate awareness. It is about acknowledging the power of these memories, the influence they have on our thoughts and actions, and the limitations they can impose.

Only by recognizing these chains can we begin to break free, to move beyond the weight of yesterday and embrace the possibilities of today.

This journey of liberation, of breaking free from the chains of the past, is not a linear one. It is a process of constant awareness, of gentle self-compassion, of embracing the present moment with open arms. It requires courage to face the painful memories, to acknowledge the impact they have had on our lives, and to choose a different path. But the journey is worth it, for it is on the other side of the chains that we discover the true potential of our being, the freedom to create a life filled with joy, love, and purpose.

Stories from the Yester

The weight of the past can be a heavy burden to carry. We all have stories that have shaped us, experiences that have left their mark on our hearts and minds. Some of these stories are beautiful, filled with the joy of childhood memories, the triumph of past successes, or the warmth of loved ones. Others are laced with pain, loss, or regret, leaving us feeling trapped in the echoes of what was.

In the tapestry of Indian culture, the past holds a profound significance. Our traditions, rituals, and values are deeply rooted in our history. It is a culture that cherishes its ancestors, reveres its heritage, and honors its legacy. This connection to the past can be a source of immense strength and guidance, but it can also become a constraint, a barrier to personal growth and the pursuit of our own unique paths.

Consider the story of **Radha**, a young woman who grew up in a traditional Indian family. Her parents, like many others, instilled in her the importance of upholding family traditions and achieving academic excellence. Radha excelled in her studies, earning a prestigious degree, and securing a high-paying job in a multinational company. On the surface, Radha seemed to have it all, fulfilling the expectations of her family and society. But beneath this facade, a sense of unease lingered within her.

Radha's heart yearned for something more, something beyond the prescribed path laid out for her. She felt a pull towards the arts, a desire to express her creativity through painting, but this longing was suppressed by the societal pressures she faced. The fear of disappointing her parents, the weight of cultural expectations, and the echoes of past failures in her artistic endeavors kept her from pursuing her true passion.

Radha 's story is not unique. Countless individuals across generations have navigated this complex interplay between cultural expectations and personal aspirations. The allure of a comfortable past, the fear of venturing into uncharted territory, and the weight of societal expectations can often overshadow our own inner desires, leading us to live a life that is not truly our own.

It is within these stories, these relatable tales of individuals caught in the past's grip, that we find the starting point for our journey of self-discovery. We can see ourselves in their struggles, their anxieties, and their yearning for something more.

Take the story of **Amit**, a man who had built a successful career as a software engineer. He had worked tirelessly, sacrificing his personal life and relationships to achieve his professional goals. He had attained the financial security he had always desired, but a profound emptiness gnawed at him.

Amit's past successes, his unwavering focus on achieving professional goals, had left him feeling disconnected from himself. His life had become a relentless pursuit of external validation, leaving him devoid of genuine joy and connection. Amit realized he had been so focused on achieving his goals that he had neglected his own needs, his own desires, and his own happiness.

The weight of Amit's past achievements, once a source of pride, now felt like a heavy chain holding him back from embracing a life of genuine fulfillment. It was a reminder that even successes, when we cling to them too tightly, can become anchors, preventing us from moving forward.

These stories highlight the complex relationship we have with our pasts. The allure of nostalgia, the yearning for a simpler time, and the comfort of past triumphs can all be compelling forces, tempting us to stay stuck in the past. But it is precisely by acknowledging the weight of our past experiences, both positive and negative, that we can begin to free ourselves from their grip and move forward with renewed purpose.

Let's explore another story, this time of **Seema**, a woman who had lost her husband to a tragic accident. The grief she experienced was profound, an overwhelming darkness that threatened to consume her.

Seema's memories of her husband, once a source of joy and comfort, now became a constant reminder of her loss. She found herself trapped in a cycle of sadness, unable to move forward. Her days were filled with a deep sense of emptiness and longing, a yearning for the comfort of the past.

It is not uncommon for those who have experienced loss to find themselves clinging to memories, trying to recapture the moments that have been lost. But these memories, though cherished, can also become a source of pain and stagnation, preventing us from healing and embracing the future.

Seema's journey was a testament to the healing power of acceptance and forgiveness. Through therapy and support from her community, she learned to navigate her grief, to honor her loss, and to gradually let go of the past. She discovered that healing wasn't about forgetting, but about finding a way to live with the memories, to integrate the pain into her life story without allowing it to define her.

Seema's journey reminds us that the past, even when filled with pain, can become a source of strength and resilience. It teaches us that the ability to confront our grief, to accept our losses, and to forgive ourselves and others is a testament to our strength and capacity for growth.

The stories of Radha, Amit, and Seema provide us with a glimpse into the complexities of navigating the past. They remind us that our past experiences, both good and bad, have a profound impact on our present lives and can either empower us or hold us back.

In the chapters that follow, we will explore the ways in which the past can affect our present and future. We will delve into the intricacies of emotional burdens, limiting beliefs, and the fear of change. We will examine the powerful tools of mindfulness, forgiveness, and gratitude that can help us break free from the chains of the past. And most importantly, we will discover the transformative power of living fully in the present moment.

2

THE IMPACTS OF DWELLING IN THE PAST

Emotional Burdens

The past is a powerful force, a tapestry woven with threads of joy, sorrow, triumph, and failure. Each experience, each emotion, leaves its mark, shaping our understanding of the world and ourselves. But while the past holds valuable lessons and cherished memories, it can also become a heavy burden, a weight that drags us down and prevents us from truly living in the present.

Imagine a beautiful, handcrafted lamp, its intricate design reflecting the artistry of its maker. But as time passes, dust settles upon its surface, obscuring its brilliance. Similarly, the past can accumulate like dust, blurring the clarity of our present experience. Unresolved feelings, like dust particles, cling to our hearts, dimming our ability to perceive the beauty and potential of the present moment.

We all carry the weight of the past in some form. It might be the lingering sting of a broken heart, the echo of a hurtful word, the shadow of a missed opportunity. These unresolved feelings can manifest as anxieties, fears, resentments, and a constant replaying of past events in our minds. They can leave us feeling trapped in a cycle of negativity, unable to move forward with a sense of lightness and freedom.

The emotional burden of the past can take various forms. It might manifest as constant worry, a nagging feeling of insecurity, or an inability to trust others. We might find ourselves struggling with low self-esteem, haunted by past mistakes, or consumed by guilt or shame. These emotions, if left unchecked, can become a heavy cloak, obscuring our vision and preventing us from truly connecting with the world around us.

For example, let's consider **Jiya**, a young woman who carries the weight of her past relationship. Her ex-partner's infidelity left her feeling betrayed and deeply hurt. She struggled to move on, fearing that every new relationship would end in the same way. Jiya's unresolved feelings created a wall around her heart, making it difficult to trust and open up to others.

Similarly, **Rahul**, a successful businessman, carries the burden of past financial failures. A series of bad investments left him with significant debt, and despite his current success, he struggles with the fear of losing everything again. Rahul's past failures have created a deep-seated anxiety that affects his decision-making and his ability to truly enjoy his accomplishments.

These are just two examples, but the emotional burdens of the past can manifest in countless ways. They can stem from childhood experiences, traumatic events, or even seemingly insignificant occurrences that have left a lasting impact. The key is to recognize that these feelings are not our present reality, but echoes from the past that we can choose to let go of.

Our cultural heritage plays a significant role in shaping our relationship with the past. In Indian culture, where family ties and tradition hold immense value, the weight of the past can be particularly pronounced. We are often taught to honor our ancestors, to carry their legacy forward, and to learn from their experiences. While this respect for our heritage is admirable, it can also lead to a tendency to cling to the past, both the good and the bad.

The cultural narrative often emphasizes the importance of learning from mistakes, but it can also lead to a cycle of guilt and self-blame. We might feel pressure to live up to the expectations of our elders, to maintain a certain reputation, or to follow in the footsteps of our ancestors. This can create a sense of obligation, a fear of disappointing those who came before us, and a reluctance to embrace change or take risks.

Moreover, Indian culture is steeped in stories of epic heroes and legendary figures, often highlighting their struggles and triumphs. While these tales provide valuable insights into our history and cultural values, they can also create a sense of comparison and inadequacy. We may find ourselves striving to live up to these idealized images, comparing our own lives and achievements to those of mythical figures, and feeling discouraged by the perceived gap.

This constant comparison can contribute to the emotional burden of the past, leading to a sense of dissatisfaction with our present lives and a yearning for a more fulfilling existence. We might find ourselves longing for the simplicity of our childhood, the carefree days of youth, or the comfort of past successes. This nostalgia, while often pleasant, can also prevent us from truly appreciating the beauty and potential of the present moment.

The cultural influence on our relationship with the past can be both a source of strength and a source of limitation. While our heritage provides us with a sense of identity and belonging, it's crucial to recognize that we are not bound by the past. We have the power to choose how we relate to our history and to shape our own narratives.

The emotional burdens of the past are real, but they do not have to define us. By acknowledging their presence, understanding their origins, and developing strategies to release their hold, we can break free from the shackles of yesterday and step into the fullness of the present moment. This journey requires courage, self-awareness, and a willingness to embrace change. It is a journey of self-discovery, of letting go, and of finding peace within ourselves. The chapters that follow will provide practical tools and insights to help you navigate this journey and reclaim your present moment.

Limiting Beliefs

The past, with all its triumphs and heartbreaks, shapes us profoundly. We carry the weight of our experiences, the echoes of past successes and failures, in our hearts and minds. These echoes, while sometimes comforting, can also cast long shadows, holding us captive to a self-limiting narrative.

Imagine a young woman named **Monali**, a budding artist in the bustling city of Mumbai. She had always dreamed of pursuing a career in art, but the path wasn't easy. Her family, grounded in traditional values, encouraged her to pursue a more stable and financially secure career, like medicine or engineering. Monali, though passionate about art, succumbed to their expectations, enrolling in a medical program. However, the years spent studying medicine felt like a constant struggle. Her heart yearned for the canvas, for the colors and forms that spoke to her soul.

Monali 's internal conflict manifested in self-doubt and limiting beliefs. The whispers of "I could have been a great artist" haunted her, gnawing at her self-esteem. Each time she picked up a brush, the memories of her unfulfilled dreams and the sacrifices she made overwhelmed her. The weight of her past choices, fueled by a deep sense of regret, imprisoned her creativity.

Monali 's story reflects a common experience. Many of us, like Monali, carry within us the echoes of past decisions, particularly those that we perceive as mistakes or failures. These past experiences, often coupled with societal expectations or cultural norms, form a complex web of beliefs that can hinder our growth and limit our potential.

Here are some common limiting beliefs that stem from dwelling on the past:

"I'm not good enough." This belief often arises from past failures, rejections, or criticisms. It can be fueled by self-doubt and a sense of inadequacy, leading to a perpetual fear of trying again. Monali, despite her passion, clung to the belief that she wasn't good enough to pursue her artistic dreams.

"I'm too old/young/unqualified." These limiting beliefs often stem from past experiences of rejection or a lack of success, leading to a sense that it's too late to pursue one's aspirations or that one lacks the necessary qualifications. A middle-aged individual who faced career setbacks might believe it's too late to make a significant change, while a young graduate might feel unqualified despite possessing the necessary skills.

"I'm not capable of change." This belief can be rooted in past failures or experiences of feeling stuck in a particular situation. It can lead to a sense of resignation and a belief that one is destined to remain in the same place. An individual who repeatedly struggled to overcome a negative habit might succumb to this belief, seeing change as an insurmountable obstacle.

"I'm destined to repeat the same mistakes." This belief arises from a pattern of negative outcomes in the past. It can lead to a sense of helplessness and a belief that one lacks control over one's actions and their future. Someone who has experienced relationship difficulties might fear repeating the same mistakes, leading to a reluctance to enter new relationships.

These limiting beliefs, often rooted in the past, can create a rigid and narrow worldview, hindering our ability to move forward. They can prevent us from embracing new opportunities, taking risks, or pursuing our passions.

<u>Breaking Free From Limiting Beliefs</u>

The good news is that these beliefs, though powerful, are not permanent. They are often learned and can be unlearned with conscious effort. Here are some strategies for challenging and overcoming these limiting beliefs:

Recognize and Challenge the Belief: The first step is to become aware of the limiting beliefs that are holding you back. Ask yourself: What beliefs am I carrying from the past? Where did these beliefs originate? How are they impacting my present life? Once you identify these beliefs, challenge their validity. Are they based on facts or on past experiences that may not be relevant to the present?

Challenge the Evidence: Often, limiting beliefs are not based on concrete evidence but on assumptions and emotional reactions. Challenge these assumptions. Consider the evidence that contradicts your beliefs. Are there examples of situations where you have overcome obstacles or achieved success?

Reframe Your Narrative: Change the story you tell yourself. Instead of focusing on past failures, focus on your strengths, your achievements, and your ability to learn from past mistakes. Embrace your resilience and your ability to grow. For Monali, this meant acknowledging her passion for art and the valuable skills she had gained through her medical education, which could be applied to her artistic endeavors.

Replace Negative Thoughts With Positive Affirmations: Positive affirmations can help you rewire your brain and create a more positive self-image. Write down affirmations that challenge your limiting beliefs. For example, instead of "I'm not good enough," try "I am capable and worthy of success."

Embrace Growth and Change: Accept that change is inevitable and that you are capable of adapting and growing. Don't view mistakes as failures but as opportunities for learning and improvement. Monali, rather than clinging to regret, embraced the idea that her medical background could enhance her artistic vision.

Seek Support and Guidance: Reach out to trusted friends, family members, mentors, or therapists. They can offer support, encouragement, and new perspectives. Monali found solace in joining an art community, where she received support from fellow artists who understood her journey.

The Power of Living in the Now

Ultimately, freeing yourself from the shackles of the past is a journey of self-discovery and liberation. It's about learning to live in the present moment, to embrace your current strengths and to seize the opportunities that lie ahead.

As we move forward, it's important to acknowledge the past without dwelling on it. We can learn from our experiences, both positive and negative, without letting them define us. The past can serve as a source of wisdom and guidance, but it should not be a prison that limits our potential. We are not bound by the choices of yesterday; we are free to create a new narrative, a future filled with possibilities.

Like Monali, who eventually found the courage to pursue her artistic dreams, each of us has the power to rewrite our stories. By challenging our limiting beliefs, embracing growth, and living fully in the present, we can free ourselves from the burdens of the past and create a life that is truly our own.

The Cost of Regret

Regret, that heavy cloak of "what ifs" and "should haves," can become a suffocating presence in our lives. It's a feeling that hangs around like a phantom, whispering doubts and insecurities, casting a shadow over our present and future. We might find ourselves constantly replaying past scenarios, wishing we had acted differently, said something differently, or made a different choice. But dwelling on these regrets only holds us captive in a cycle of negativity.

Imagine a young woman named **Lakshmi**, a bright and talented artist who dreamt of opening her own gallery. But fear held her back, a fear rooted in the past. Years ago, she had poured her heart and soul into a project, only to have it rejected, leaving her feeling deeply discouraged. This past experience cast a long shadow over her aspirations, and Lakshmi found herself hesitant to take the leap again. She allowed the sting of the past rejection to define her potential, convincing herself that she wasn't good enough, that she would only face more disappointment.

Lakshmi 's story is a familiar one. We all carry the baggage of our past experiences, and sometimes, it's the negative ones that seem to linger the longest. They become our "go-to" stories, the ones we tell ourselves to justify our inaction, our fear, our reluctance to step outside our comfort zones. We might tell ourselves, "I've been hurt before, so I'm going to protect myself from further pain," or "I've failed once, so I'm going to avoid taking risks altogether."

The problem with these narratives, however, is that they hold us hostage to our past. We become prisoners of our own memories, unable to see the possibilities that lie before us. Regret steals our present joy, our ability to experience the beauty of the now, and our confidence to embrace the future. It's like carrying a heavy weight on our shoulders, preventing us from moving forward, from living life to the fullest.

The cost of regret is immense. It robs us of precious opportunities, stifles our personal growth, and limits our capacity for happiness. When we choose to dwell on our regrets, we choose to miss out on the abundance of possibilities that life offers. We miss out on:

New experiences: Every moment offers a chance for something new, something exciting, something that can spark our passions and light our way. But if we are constantly looking back, we miss out on the wonders that are happening in the present.

Learning and growth: Life is a constant journey of learning, of evolving, of becoming more than we were yesterday. Regret hinders this growth by focusing us on past mistakes instead of present opportunities.

Resilience and strength: By letting go of regret, we empower ourselves to face challenges with a stronger, more resilient spirit. We learn from our mistakes, we acknowledge our strengths, and we move forward with the confidence that we can overcome any obstacle.

Authentic connections: Regret can isolate us, turning us inward and creating emotional distance from others. When we choose to let go of the past, we open ourselves up to deeper, more fulfilling connections with the people around us.

The path to releasing the grip of regret is not always easy. It requires a willingness to confront our past, to acknowledge our mistakes, and to forgive ourselves and others. It requires courage to step outside our comfort zones, to embrace change, and to believe in our potential to create a brighter future.

Think of a young man named **Amar**, a gifted musician who dreamed of performing on stage. But fear held him back, a fear rooted in a past experience where his first public performance was met with lukewarm reception. The criticism he received had left a lasting impact, a sense of inadequacy that clung to him. Amar continued to practice his craft, but he never dared to share his music with the world. He convinced himself that he wasn't good enough, that he would only be met with rejection again.

Amar's story highlights how regret can create a self-fulfilling prophecy. By constantly dwelling on past failures, we can create a negative mindset that actually inhibits our ability to succeed. We become so focused on avoiding past mistakes that we fail to see the opportunities for growth and achievement that lie ahead.

Releasing the grip of regret doesn't mean erasing the past or pretending it never happened. It means learning from it, growing from it, and moving on from it. It means choosing to focus on the present moment, on the possibilities that lie before us, and on the potential, we have to create a life filled with joy, purpose, and fulfillment.

Here are some practical strategies to help you release the grip of regret:

Practice gratitude: Take time each day to appreciate the good things in your life, both big and small. This shifts your focus from what you lack to what you have, fostering a more positive outlook.

Acknowledge your feelings: Don't try to suppress or ignore your regrets. Allow yourself to feel the emotions that come with them, but don't dwell on them. Recognize that these emotions are part of your human experience, and they will pass.

Learn from your mistakes: Instead of replaying past events, ask yourself, "What can I learn from this experience?" Focus on the lessons you can take away from your mistakes and how they can help you grow.

Forgive yourself and others: Holding onto anger, resentment, and blame only perpetuates the cycle of negativity. Forgive yourself for your mistakes and others for their actions. Release the burden of holding onto these emotions.

Focus on the present: Practice mindfulness. Engage with the present moment, with your senses, with your thoughts and feelings. Be fully present in each experience, rather than reliving the past.

Visualize your future: Imagine yourself achieving your goals, living a fulfilling life, and experiencing joy and peace. This helps you shift your focus from the past to the future you are creating.

The past is a part of our story, but it does not define our entire narrative. We have the power to rewrite our story, to create a future filled with hope, opportunity, and joy. Let go of the burdens of regret and embrace the present moment. It is in the here and now that we can truly live, create, and fulfill our potential.

Release the chains of regret. Embrace the power of the present. You are capable of creating a future filled with possibilities. Remember, the journey of life is not about reliving yesterday, but about creating a better tomorrow.

The Fear of Change

The fear of change is a powerful and pervasive force that can stem from our past experiences. It's the voice in our head that whispers, "Don't try something new, you'll only get hurt again." This fear often arises from the pain of past failures, the sting of rejections, or the deep grief of losses. These experiences, etched into our memory, can create a sense of vulnerability towards the unknown, making us hesitant to venture beyond the familiar, even if it means missing out on potential growth and happiness.

Imagine a young woman named **Rani**, who had always dreamt of being a writer. But in her youth, she had faced rejection after rejection from publishers, each one chipping away at her confidence. These experiences left her with a deep-seated fear of failure, a fear that manifested as a reluctance to even try again. Years passed, and Rani remained stuck in a monotonous job, her dream of writing relegated to a distant memory. The past had become a prison, its bars forged from fear and self-doubt.

However, Maya's story is not unique. Many of us, like Rani, carry within us the weight of past experiences that cast a shadow over our present and future. This is especially true in cultures like India, where tradition and the expectations of family and society often create a pressure to conform and stay within the bounds of the familiar. The fear of disappointing loved ones, the fear of societal judgment, and the fear of venturing into the unknown can be paralyzing.

This fear of change is often reinforced by our own limiting beliefs. Past failures, even if they were small or insignificant, can become ingrained in our minds, shaping our perception of ourselves and our capabilities. We start to believe that we are not good enough, that we are not meant for success, or that we are destined to repeat the mistakes of the past. These limiting beliefs become self-fulfilling prophecies, trapping us in a cycle of inaction and preventing us from embracing new opportunities.

But the past, while it has a profound impact, does not have to define us. It is important to remember that past experiences, both positive and negative, are simply lessons learned along the way. They are not meant to hold us back, but to guide us towards a brighter future. We can choose to use our past experiences as fuel for growth, as reminders of our resilience, and as sources of wisdom.

Imagine a young man named **Rohan**, who had experienced the devastating loss of his father at a young age. This loss left him with deep-seated grief and a fear of losing other loved ones. As a result, Rohan avoided close relationships and kept his emotions at bay, fearing that vulnerability would only lead to more pain. He lived a life of isolation, fearing that any connection would ultimately end in heartbreak.

However, Rohan's story, like Seema's, also represents a turning point. Through therapy and the support of friends, Rohan began to understand that his fear was stemming from his past loss. He realized that his avoidance of closeness was not protecting him from pain, but rather preventing him from experiencing the beauty and joy of true connection. With the support of his therapist and his friends, Rohan began to take small steps towards opening his heart. He started making new connections, nurturing friendships, and allowing himself to be vulnerable.

Just as Rohan learned to face his fear of vulnerability, we can all learn to confront the fear of change that holds us back. It begins with recognizing the power of our past experiences, acknowledging the emotions and beliefs that they have shaped, and understanding how those emotions and beliefs are impacting our present lives.

One key to overcoming the fear of change is to cultivate a growth mindset. This means approaching new experiences with a sense of curiosity and openness, rather than fear and resistance. It means believing in our ability to learn, adapt, and grow, even in the face of challenges.

The journey of personal growth is a lifelong one, filled with both triumphs and setbacks. Each experience, both positive and negative, can teach us something about ourselves and the world around us. It is by learning from our past, embracing our present, and envisioning a brighter future that we can truly break free from the constraints of yesterday and step confidently into the unknown.

Our past experiences have shaped us into the individuals we are today, but they do not have to define our future. We can choose to learn from our mistakes, to celebrate our successes, and to use our past as a springboard for growth. We can choose to embrace change, to step outside of our comfort zones, and to create a life that is filled with joy, purpose, and fulfillment.

Here are some practical steps we can take to overcome the fear of change and embrace a life of growth:

1. Acknowledge and Validate Your Feelings: Begin by acknowledging and validating the feelings that arise from past experiences. Instead of suppressing or dismissing them, allow yourself to feel them fully. Recognize that your feelings are valid and that they are a part of your journey.

2. Challenge Limiting Beliefs: Identify the limiting beliefs that are holding you back from taking risks and embracing change. Ask yourself: "Where did these beliefs come from? Are they really true? Are they serving me?" Challenge these beliefs by replacing them with more empowering thoughts.

3. Practice Mindfulness: Mindfulness is a powerful tool that can help you become more aware of your thoughts, feelings, and sensations in the present moment. By cultivating mindfulness, you can reduce the grip of past experiences on your present and create more space for joy and freedom.

4. Embrace Forgiveness: Forgiveness, both for others and for yourself, is essential for moving on from the past. Forgiving those who have hurt you releases you from the chains of resentment and allows you to move forward with a lighter heart. Forgiving yourself for past mistakes allows you to break free from guilt and shame, enabling you to embrace new opportunities with confidence.

5. Cultivate a Growth Mindset: A growth mindset is characterized by a belief in your ability to learn and grow. It means embracing challenges as opportunities for development and viewing setbacks as learning experiences. By fostering a growth mindset, you can unlock your potential and achieve your dreams.

6. Set Small, Achievable Goals: Break down larger goals into smaller, more manageable steps. Celebrate each small victory along the way, building momentum and confidence as you progress.

7. Seek Support: Surround yourself with supportive individuals who believe in you and encourage your growth. Reach out to friends, family, or a therapist for guidance and support on your journey.

8. Embrace the Journey: The path to personal growth is not always easy, but it is always rewarding. Remember that you are not alone in this journey, and that every step you take, even the small ones, brings you closer to your potential.

By understanding the roots of the fear of change, embracing a growth mindset, and implementing practical strategies for personal growth, you can rewrite your narrative, create a fulfilling future, and ultimately live a life free from the constraints of yesterday. You can choose to live fully in the present, embracing each moment with joy, purpose, and a deep sense of inner peace.

Case Studies of Stagnation

The past can be a powerful force, shaping our thoughts, beliefs, and behaviors. It can also be a source of great pain and regret, especially when we fail to acknowledge the negative impact it has on our present lives.

One of the most significant effects of dwelling in the past is stagnation. We become trapped in a cycle of rumination, replaying past events, reliving old emotions, and refusing to move forward. This can manifest in various ways, impacting our personal relationships, careers, and overall well-being.

Case Study 1: The Weight of Unforgiveness
Meet **Avnai**, a successful businesswoman who, despite her achievements, carried the weight of a past heartbreak. Years ago, her fiancé had broken off their engagement, leaving her devastated and questioning her self-worth. While she had seemingly moved on, the deep-seated pain of rejection lingered. Avnai's inability to forgive her ex-fiancé manifested in several ways. She found it difficult to trust new partners, fearing the same pain. She constantly compared her current relationships to the lost love, finding flaws and deficiencies. This constant comparison and mistrust made it challenging for her to build lasting connections and experience true happiness.

Case Study 2: The Grip of Past Failures
Rajesh, a talented artist, struggled to find his place in the art world. He had initially enjoyed great success with his paintings, receiving recognition and selling his work at prestigious galleries. However, his career took a downturn when his art was criticized harshly by a renowned art critic. The harsh criticism, coupled with his own insecurities, led to a period of self-doubt and creative block. Rajesh retreated from the art scene, fearing rejection and unable to overcome the fear of facing another critique. He constantly revisited the scathing critique, allowing it to define his artistic abilities and hold him back from pursuing his passion.

Case Study 3: The Curse of Missed Opportunities
Simran was a promising young entrepreneur who had to abandon her dream business venture after a major financial setback. Despite the success of her initial venture, unforeseen circumstances led to a loss of investment and forced her to close shop. The financial burden and the feeling of failure weighed heavily on Simran. She found herself constantly replaying the events leading to her business's demise, feeling trapped by the mistakes she made. This constant dwelling on the past hindered her ability to envision new opportunities and to take risks necessary for building

a new venture.

The Consequences of Stagnation
These case studies illustrate how dwelling in the past can lead to a cycle of stagnation, affecting our emotional well-being, limiting our growth, and hindering our ability to embrace new possibilities.

Emotional Burdens: The unresolved emotions and feelings from the past become like heavy anchors, dragging us down and preventing us from experiencing true peace and joy in the present.

Limiting Beliefs: Past failures, disappointments, and experiences shape our beliefs about ourselves and the world around us. These beliefs, often negative and limiting, can hinder our progress and prevent us from achieving our full potential.

Fear of Change: The past can become a comfort zone, even when it's filled with pain. We may fear change because we are afraid of repeating past mistakes or encountering similar disappointments.

The Cost of Regret: Regretting past choices and actions can be emotionally draining and hinder our ability to make positive choices in the present. It can also prevent us from pursuing new opportunities, fearing similar outcomes.

Missed Opportunities: By fixating on what could have been or what we have lost, we miss out on the opportunities and experiences that are available to us now. We are unable to fully embrace the present, and we miss the chance to create a brighter future.

Breaking Free from the Past
The key to breaking free from the past is to understand the root cause of our stagnation. This requires introspection, self-awareness, and a willingness to confront our fears and limiting beliefs. The journey towards liberation is a personal one, and it demands honesty, courage, and a commitment to growth.

The following chapters will provide practical strategies and techniques to help you navigate the complexities of the past, release its grip, and embrace the transformative power of the present moment. We will explore the art of mindfulness, the importance of forgiveness, and the power of rewriting our narratives. By recognizing the impact of the past and taking proactive steps to move forward, we can unlock our true potential and create a life filled with purpose, joy, and fulfillment.

3

EMBRACING THE PRESENT MOMENT

The Art of Mindfulness

The present moment, that fleeting instant where time stands still, is often overlooked in our relentless pursuit of the future or our preoccupation with the past. We chase deadlines, dwell on regrets, and dream of distant shores, all the while neglecting the richness of the now. Yet, it is in this very moment, this seemingly insignificant point in time, that life unfolds its tapestry of experiences, emotions, and possibilities.

Mindfulness, a practice deeply rooted in ancient Indian wisdom, offers a key to unlocking the treasure trove of the present. It is the art of cultivating awareness, of being fully present in each breath, each thought, each sensation. It's about observing our thoughts, feelings, and bodily sensations without judgment, allowing them to simply be. This gentle practice can help us break free from the chains of the past, quell the anxiety of the future, and savor the beauty of the present.

Imagine a bustling marketplace, teeming with vibrant colors, enticing aromas, and the lively chatter of vendors. A typical response might be to rush through, our minds preoccupied with a shopping list, oblivious to the symphony of sounds and the intricate details of the scene. However, with mindfulness, we can pause, take a deep breath, and truly experience the marketplace. We can observe the intricate patterns on a silk scarf, the delicate dance of smoke from a street vendor's grill, the warmth of the sun on our skin. We are present, fully engaged in the moment, appreciating the richness of the experience.

Mindfulness isn't just about appreciating the beauty of our surroundings; it's about deepening our understanding of ourselves. It's about recognizing the subtle shifts in our emotions, noticing the subtle tension in our shoulders, or the flutter of excitement in our chest. By paying attention to our internal landscape, we gain valuable insights into our patterns of thought and behavior, allowing us to cultivate greater self-awareness and emotional intelligence.

There are countless ways to cultivate mindfulness, each tailored to individual preferences and needs. Simple practices like mindful breathing, where we focus on the rise and fall of our breath, can create a sense of calm and centeredness. Mindful walking, where we pay attention to the sensations of our feet on the ground, the rhythm of our steps, and the changing scenery, can help us connect with the present moment. Mindful eating, where we savor each bite, paying attention to the textures, flavors, and aromas, can enhance our appreciation for the simple pleasures of life.

One powerful tool for cultivating mindfulness is meditation. Meditation isn't about emptying our minds; it's about training our attention to stay focused on the present moment. We can sit quietly, focusing on our breath, observing our thoughts without judgment, allowing them to flow like clouds across the sky. Regular meditation practice can help us develop a greater sense of inner peace, emotional resilience, and mental clarity.

As we cultivate mindfulness, we begin to see the world with fresh eyes, appreciating the beauty in the ordinary. We find joy in the simple act of drinking our morning tea, in the warmth of the sun on our face, in the laughter of a loved one. We learn to release attachments to past experiences, recognizing that they are simply memories, not defining elements of who we are.

Imagine a woman named **Rekha**, burdened by the weight of a painful childhood experience. Memories of betrayal and neglect replayed constantly in her mind, casting a shadow over her present. She felt trapped, unable to move forward. Through mindfulness practice, Rekha learned to observe her thoughts and emotions without judgment. She noticed the familiar tightening in her chest, the familiar wave of sadness, and she simply allowed them to be without resistance. Slowly, she began to detach from the emotional grip of the past, finding solace in the present moment.

Mindfulness doesn't erase the past, nor does it deny the reality of our experiences. Instead, it provides a space to process those experiences with compassion, to understand their influence on our present without being consumed by them. It allows us to reclaim our power, to step out of the shadows of the past and embrace the boundless possibilities of the present.

Mindfulness is a journey, not a destination. It's a practice that requires patience, persistence, and a willingness to be present, to observe, and to let go. It's about accepting the ebb and flow of life, the joy and the sorrow, the triumphs and the setbacks, all within the context of the present moment. It's about living a life that is not defined by the past, but shaped by the choices we make in this very moment.

As we navigate the complexities of life, embracing the present moment through the practice of mindfulness can be a guiding light, leading us towards a life of greater clarity, inner peace, and fulfillment. It's a journey of self-discovery, a path to liberation from the shackles of the past, and a step towards creating a present and a future filled with meaning and purpose.

Cultivating Awareness

The journey to truly living in the present starts with cultivating awareness. It's about tuning into the subtle symphony of our experiences, noticing the sensations, thoughts, and emotions that dance through us in every moment. This heightened awareness isn't about striving for perfection or achieving some idealized state of serenity; it's about acknowledging the richness and complexity of our inner world, without judgment or resistance.

Imagine a river flowing swiftly, carrying with it the stories of its journey. We are like that river, constantly moving, ever-changing, carrying the weight of our past and the anticipation of our future. Yet so often we get caught up in the rapids of our minds, lost in the swirling currents of thoughts and emotions. We dwell on yesterday's regrets, worry about tomorrow's uncertainties, and fail to fully embrace the present moment.

Cultivating awareness is about stepping back from the rushing currents and observing the river itself. It's about acknowledging the sensations of the cool water against our skin, the gentle swaying of the reeds along the bank, the melodic gurgle as the water flows over rocks. It's about noticing the quiet beauty of the present, the subtle nuances that often get overlooked in our preoccupation with the past and the future.

Here are some practical exercises to help you cultivate awareness of your current experiences and emotions:

1. The Body Scan: This is a simple yet powerful technique that helps you connect with your physical sensations. Find a comfortable place to sit or lie down, closing your eyes if you feel comfortable doing so. Start by bringing your attention to your breath, noticing the gentle rise and fall of your chest or belly. Then, slowly shift your attention to your toes, feeling the sensations of pressure and temperature. Gradually move your awareness up your body, noticing the sensations in your feet, ankles, calves, and so on.

Pay attention to any tightness, tingling, warmth, or coolness you experience. If you notice your mind wandering, gently bring it back to your body. The key is to observe without judgment, simply noticing the sensations as they are. You can practice this for a few minutes each day, gradually increasing the duration as you become more comfortable with the practice.

2. The Five Senses Exercise: This exercise encourages you to engage all of your senses, bringing you fully into the present moment. Find a quiet place where you can focus for a few minutes. Start by closing your eyes and focusing on your breath, noticing the sensation of the air moving in and out of your nostrils.

Then, slowly open your eyes and bring your attention to your surroundings. Observe the colors, shapes, and textures around you. Notice the scent of the air, whether it's the aroma of fresh coffee, the scent of blooming flowers, or the subtle earthy smell of the soil. Listen to the sounds around you, perhaps the chirping of birds, the rustling of leaves, or the hum of traffic in the distance. Taste the subtle flavors on your tongue, even if it's just the taste of your own saliva.

This exercise can be done anywhere, anytime, reminding you to be present in your surroundings and appreciate the simple sensory experiences that make up our lives.

3. Mindful Walking: Many of us walk through life with our minds racing, lost in thought, failing to truly experience the act of walking itself. Mindful walking allows us to savor the simple pleasure of moving our bodies, connecting with our surroundings in a more conscious way.

Find a quiet place where you can walk without distractions, a park, a nature trail, or even your own backyard. Begin by focusing on the sensation of your feet touching the ground, the feeling of the air against your skin, the rhythm of your breath. Notice the subtle movements of your body, the swinging of your arms, the gentle sway of your hips.

Pay attention to your surroundings, observing the colors, shapes, and textures around you. Notice the sounds of birds chirping, leaves rustling, or the gentle murmur of a nearby stream. As you walk, try to maintain a gentle awareness of your body and your surroundings, allowing yourself to be fully present in the moment.

4. Mindful Eating: Eating is often a hurried, mindless activity, a way to fuel our bodies without truly appreciating the experience. Mindful eating allows us to savor each bite, connecting with the tastes, textures, and smells of our food.

Before you begin eating, take a moment to observe your food. Notice its colors, shapes, and textures. Smell its aroma, allowing the scent to fill your senses. As you eat, pay attention to the taste of each bite, noticing the subtle nuances of flavors and textures. Chew your food slowly, savoring each mouthful.

Notice the sensations in your mouth, the feeling of the food passing through your throat. Observe any thoughts or emotions that arise while you are eating. It is helpful to put away distractions like your phone or television, creating a space of quiet focus on the simple act of eating.

5. Journaling: Writing down your thoughts and emotions can be a powerful tool for cultivating awareness. Set aside some time each day to journal, allowing yourself to freely express whatever comes to mind. Don't worry about grammar or spelling; simply let your thoughts flow onto the page.

Write about your experiences, both positive and negative. Reflect on your emotions, noticing any patterns or recurring themes. Write about your goals, dreams, and aspirations.

Journaling can help you become more aware of your inner world, providing a space for self-reflection and exploration. It can also be a valuable tool for releasing pent-up emotions, processing difficult experiences, and fostering self-compassion.

6. Meditation: Meditation is a time-honored practice for cultivating awareness and quieting the mind. It involves sitting or lying down in a comfortable position, focusing on your breath, and observing your thoughts and emotions without judgment.

You can begin with short meditation sessions of 5-10 minutes each day, gradually increasing the duration as you become more comfortable. There are many guided meditation resources available online and in libraries.

Meditation can help you develop greater awareness of your thoughts, feelings, and bodily sensations. It can also help you cultivate a sense of calm and inner peace, reducing stress and promoting emotional well-being.

7. Nature Walks: The natural world offers a rich tapestry of sensory experiences, inviting us to step away from the demands of daily life and immerse ourselves in the present moment. Take a walk in a park, a forest, or along the beach, allowing yourself to be fully present in your surroundings.

Notice the colors, shapes, and textures of the natural world. Listen to the sounds of birds singing, leaves rustling, or waves crashing on the shore. Breathe in the fresh air, allowing its scent to fill your lungs. As you walk, try to observe your thoughts and emotions, noticing any patterns or recurring themes.

Nature walks can be a powerful way to cultivate awareness, offering a sense of peace and grounding that can help you return to your daily life with a renewed sense of presence.

These exercises are just a starting point. Experiment with different approaches, find what resonates with you, and be patient with yourself. The journey of cultivating awareness is a lifelong process, filled with both challenges and rewards. As you become more attuned to your present experiences, you'll discover a newfound sense of peace, clarity, and joy. The world around you will seem more vibrant, your relationships more meaningful, and your life more fulfilling.

Remember, the present moment is a gift, a precious opportunity to experience the beauty and wonder of life. By cultivating awareness, you can learn to savor each moment, releasing the grip of the past and embracing the possibilities of the present.

Releasing Attachments

Releasing the grip of the past is like loosening a knot that has tightened over time. It requires patience, practice, and a willingness to let go. Just as a sculptor chip away at stone to reveal a masterpiece, we must chip away at the layers of emotional attachments that hold us captive.

One powerful technique is to practice **Mindfulness**. It's about focusing on the present moment, without judgment, and observing our thoughts and feelings as they arise. Imagine yourself sitting by a serene river, watching the water flow by, without trying to control it. This is the essence of mindfulness—allowing thoughts and feelings to come and go without getting swept away by them.

Mindful breathing is a simple yet effective way to cultivate presence. Sit comfortably, close your eyes, and focus on the rise and fall of your breath. Notice the sensation of air entering and leaving your nostrils. As you focus on your breath, you may find thoughts and feelings arise. Acknowledge them without judgment, and gently guide your attention back to your breath.

Journaling can be a powerful tool for releasing emotional attachments. Writing down your thoughts and feelings can help you process them and gain a deeper understanding of their origins. Imagine releasing your anxieties and worries onto the pages of your journal, allowing them to flow out and dissipate.

Meditation is another way to cultivate mindfulness and let go of past attachments. It's a practice of quieting the mind and focusing on the present moment. Find a quiet space, sit comfortably, and close your eyes. Focus on your breath, or a mantra, or simply observe the sensations of your body. With regular practice, meditation can help you develop a greater sense of peace and clarity.

Visualisation is a technique that uses imagery to create a desired state of being. Imagine yourself in a peaceful setting, surrounded by nature or loved ones. Visualise yourself breathing deeply, feeling calm and relaxed. Imagine the past events that are causing you distress fading away, replaced by a sense of peace and acceptance.

Gratitude practice is another powerful tool for letting go of the past. When we focus on the good things in our lives, we shift our attention away from the negative and create a more positive mindset. Start a gratitude journal and write down three things you are grateful for each day. This simple act can help you shift your perspective and focus on the present moment.

Forgiveness is a crucial aspect of releasing attachments. It's not about condoning the actions of others, but about freeing ourselves from the burden of resentment and anger. Holding on to anger only harms ourselves. Forgiveness allows us to release the emotional weight of the past and move forward with a lighter heart.

Acceptance is key to letting go. Accept that the past is in the past, and we cannot change it. Trying to hold onto the past only keeps us stuck. Accept the present moment as it is, without judgment. Embrace the good, the bad, and the ugly. This acceptance allows us to move forward with a sense of peace and clarity.

Surrender is about releasing control and trusting in a higher power. This can be a difficult concept to grasp, but it's essential for letting go of attachments. We often cling to the past because we feel a need to control our experiences. Surrendering to the unknown can be liberating. It allows us to trust in the process of life and accept what is.

Remember, releasing attachments is a journey, not a destination. It's a process that requires patience, persistence, and compassion for ourselves. There will be times when we slip back into old patterns, but it's important to acknowledge these moments without judgment and gently guide ourselves back to the present.

Here are some additional tips for releasing attachments:

Identify the root cause of your attachment: What specific event or experience is holding you back? Understanding the source of your attachment can help you address it more effectively.

Challenge your limiting beliefs: Are there any negative beliefs about yourself or the world that are stemming from your past? Challenge these beliefs and replace them with more positive and empowering ones.

Seek professional help: If you are struggling to release attachments on your own, consider seeking guidance from a therapist or counselor. They can provide support and tools to help you navigate your journey.

Practice self-compassion: Be kind and understanding to yourself. Everyone makes mistakes, and it's okay to struggle. Treat yourself with the same compassion you would offer to a loved one.

Releasing attachments is a powerful act of self-love and liberation. It allows us to break free from the chains of the past and embrace the freedom and joy of the present moment. It's a journey of self-discovery that can lead to a more fulfilling and authentic life.

The Joy of Now

Imagine a gentle breeze caressing your skin, the warmth of the sun on your face, the sweet fragrance of jasmine wafting through the air. These are the sensations of the present moment, a realm often overlooked in our relentless pursuit of yesterday's echoes and tomorrow's promises. Yet, it is in the embrace of the present that true joy and fulfillment reside.

The present moment is not a static, fleeting point in time; it is a continuous flow of experience, a tapestry woven with the threads of our thoughts, emotions, and senses. It is a symphony of life unfolding, a kaleidoscope of sights, sounds, and feelings that paint a unique and ever-changing portrait of existence. When we allow ourselves to fully inhabit the present moment, we unlock a reservoir of peace and contentment that surpasses the fleeting pleasures of dwelling in the past or anxiously anticipating the future.

The joy of the present moment is not merely a passive experience; it is an active choice we make to engage with life with full presence and appreciation. It requires a conscious shift in our perspective, a deliberate decision to relinquish the grip of past regrets and future anxieties. It is a journey of cultivating awareness, embracing the beauty of the ordinary, and recognizing the gifts that each moment holds.

Think of it as a child's unfettered delight in a simple game of tag, their senses fully absorbed in the thrill of the chase, their laughter echoing the pure joy of being alive. Or consider the serenity found in a quiet moment of meditation, the mind still, the body relaxed, the soul bathed in the tranquility of the present. These moments, however fleeting, offer a glimpse into the richness of living fully in the now.

The practice of mindfulness is an essential tool for cultivating this present moment awareness. Mindfulness is the art of paying attention, without judgment, to the unfolding experience of the moment. It is about noticing the sensations of our body, the thoughts that arise in our mind, and the emotions that ripple through us, without getting carried away by them. It is about observing our thoughts, feelings, and sensations with curiosity and acceptance, without resisting or clinging to them.

There are numerous ways to cultivate mindfulness, from formal meditation practices to simple everyday techniques. A few examples include:

Mindful Breathing: Focus on your breath, observing the natural rhythm of inhalation and exhalation. Notice the subtle sensations of the air entering and leaving your nostrils, the expansion and contraction of your chest.

Mindful Walking: Pay attention to the sensations of your feet on the ground, the movement of your legs, and the rhythm of your steps. Notice the sights, sounds, and smells that surround you.

Mindful Eating: Engage all your senses as you eat. Notice the color, texture, and aroma of your food. Take small bites, savor each mouthful, and chew thoroughly. Pay attention to the taste and the sensations in your mouth.

As you practice mindfulness, you will begin to notice the subtle shifts in your awareness. You will start to become more present in your daily life, less preoccupied with the past or the future. You will discover a renewed appreciation for the simple joys of existence, the beauty of a sunrise, the warmth of a hug, the comfort of a cup of tea.

This shift in perspective, this embrace of the present, can bring about profound transformations in our lives. It can dissolve the anxieties that gnaw at us, replace the regrets that haunt us, and cultivate a sense of contentment and gratitude for the life we are living. It can unlock creativity, enhance our relationships, and empower us to live more authentically.

The joy of the present moment is a treasure waiting to be discovered. It is not something that is achieved through willpower alone; it is a practice, a journey that requires patience, perseverance, and a willingness to let go of the past and embrace the infinite possibilities of the now.

It is a journey that begins with a single breath, a moment of mindful awareness. With each step, with each mindful breath, we move closer to the heart of our being, the source of true happiness and fulfillment. The journey begins now.

Mindful Living Examples

In the heart of bustling Mumbai, amidst the cacophony of honking autos and vibrant street markets, lived a woman named **Mira**. Once a successful entrepreneur, she had experienced a devastating business failure that left her drowning in debt and shattered confidence. Mira's days were filled with the echoes of her past mistakes, replaying in her mind like a broken record. Each morning started with a heavy heart, burdened by the weight of what could have been, and each night ended with the bitter sting of regret.

She found herself lost in a labyrinth of "what ifs" and "should haves." "If only I had taken that loan," she'd think, or "If only I had listened to my instincts." This constant dwelling on the past had consumed her present, leaving little room for joy, hope, or even the possibility of a fresh start. Every interaction, every conversation felt tainted by the shadow of her failure.

Mira's friends, concerned by her withdrawn demeanor, tried to offer support and encouragement, but she found it difficult to accept. "I've made such a mess of my life," she'd say, her voice tinged with despair. "It's all my fault." Her past mistakes had become her identity, a label she wore with a sense of shame and resignation.

One evening, as Mira sat alone in her dimly lit apartment, staring at the remnants of a failed business venture, a book titled "Living in the Present: Finding Peace in the Now" caught her eye. It had been a gift from a well-meaning friend, but Mira had pushed it aside, feeling that such concepts were irrelevant to her current state. But with a quiet desperation gnawing at her, she picked it up and began to read.

The book introduced the concept of mindfulness, a practice rooted in ancient Eastern wisdom. It spoke about the power of focusing our attention on the present moment, without judgment or attachment to the past or future. It emphasized the importance of being fully present in each breath, each experience, each interaction.

At first, Mira was skeptical. How could simply paying attention to the present alleviate her pain? How could it erase the memories of her failures? But the book also spoke of the transformative power of mindfulness, of how it could create a sense of peace and acceptance, even in the midst of suffering.

Intrigued, Mira decided to give it a try. She began with a simple exercise – focusing on her breath. She closed her eyes and inhaled deeply, feeling the air fill her lungs, and exhaled slowly, releasing the tension she carried within. At first, her thoughts drifted back to her past failures, but with each breath, she gently nudged them aside, bringing her attention back to the present moment.

As she continued to practice mindfulness throughout the day, Mira began to notice subtle shifts. She started to appreciate the simple pleasures of a cup of chai in the morning sun, the warmth of a friend's hug, the soothing rhythm of the city around her. She found herself less consumed by the past and more open to the present.

One morning, as she walked to the market, Mira noticed a young boy selling flowers. He was no older than eight, but his smile was infectious, his eyes full of hope. As she bought a bouquet, she felt a surge of warmth, a sense of connection that had been absent for so long.

Later that day, a friend invited Mira to a networking event, an event she would have normally avoided, burdened by her past failures. But something within her had shifted. She found herself accepting the invitation, a small flicker of curiosity replacing the overwhelming fear.

At the event, Mira met a seasoned entrepreneur who shared his own journey of setbacks and triumphs. He spoke about the importance of learning from mistakes and embracing the challenges that come with growth. His words resonated with Mira, offering a new perspective on her own experience.

Inspired by this encounter, Priya began to see her past failures not as a source of shame but as valuable lessons. She started to view her current situation as an opportunity for growth and reinvention. With newfound determination, she began to explore new business ideas, focusing on her strengths and passions.

As Mira's journey unfolded, she discovered the profound impact of mindfulness on her life. It wasn't a quick fix; it was a continuous practice that required commitment and effort. But with each mindful breath, each conscious moment, she felt a sense of inner peace, a release from the shackles of the past, and a newfound appreciation for the present.

Mira's story, like the stories of countless others, demonstrates the transformative power of embracing the present moment. It reminds us that while the past may have shaped us, it doesn't define us. By cultivating mindfulness, we can break free from the chains of our past, find solace in the present, and create a brighter future.

The journey from dwelling in the past to living fully in the present is not always easy. It requires a willingness to let go, to embrace vulnerability, and to trust in the transformative power of the present moment. But as Mira discovered, the rewards are immeasurable, a sense of peace, a renewed sense of purpose, and the freedom to truly live life to the fullest.

This is not just Mira's story. This is the story of countless individuals across India and around the world who have found liberation through mindfulness. It is the story of the young artist who, haunted by his past failures, found solace in the rhythm of his brushstrokes, rediscovering the joy of creation in the present moment. It is the story of the middle-aged woman, burdened by the weight of societal expectations, who found her voice through the ancient practice of yoga, reclaiming her strength and agency. It is the story of the elderly gentleman, grappling with the loss of a loved one, who found comfort in the simplicity of a daily walk in nature, rediscovering the beauty and wonder of the present moment.

These are just a few examples of how embracing the present moment can transform lives. It's not about erasing the past, but about recognizing its lessons and moving forward with a renewed sense of purpose. It's about finding joy in the simple things, appreciating the people in our lives, and embracing the beauty of each passing moment.

In the wisdom of the **Bhagavad Gita**, we find the words, "This is the moment, my friend, this is the time, this is the only time you have." These words hold a profound truth – the only moment we truly have is the present moment. It is in this moment that we can find peace, joy, and fulfillment. It is in this moment that we can truly live.

And so, as we navigate the complexities of life, let us remember the importance of living in the present. Let us cultivate mindfulness, let go of the past, and embrace the transformative power of the now. For in the present moment, we find not just peace, but a profound sense of freedom, the freedom to create a life that is truly our own.

4

THE PATH TO FORGIVENESS

<u>Understanding Forgiveness</u>

Forgiveness, a word that often carries a heavy weight, is not just a concept relegated to religious texts or philosophical treatises. It is a powerful tool for personal liberation, a bridge that allows us to navigate the turbulent waters of our past, ultimately leading us to a calmer, more peaceful shore.

Imagine a river flowing steadily toward the ocean. Along its course, there are rocks, obstacles that disrupt its flow. These rocks are like the wounds we carry from our past - the hurtful words, the broken promises, the failures that leave scars on our hearts. We hold on to these wounds, letting them fester and poison our present moment. We become trapped in a cycle of resentment, anger, and pain, unable to move forward freely.

But what if we could somehow remove those rocks? What if we could find a way to dissolve the pain of the past, to release the grip it has on our hearts? This is where forgiveness enters the picture.

Forgiveness isn't about condoning or forgetting the hurt. It's not about minimizing the pain or dismissing the injustice. Forgiveness is a choice, a conscious decision to release the bitterness, the anger, and the resentment that keep us bound to the past. It's about choosing to break free from the shackles of pain and allowing ourselves to move forward.

Think of it like this: forgiveness is like letting go of a heavy burden. It's about releasing the weight of the past and allowing yourself to feel lighter, freer. It's about making peace with the past, not for the sake of the person who hurt you, but for your own peace of mind.

Forgiving others is a crucial step in this process. It's about recognizing that everyone makes mistakes, that everyone is flawed, and that we all have the capacity for both good and bad actions. It's about understanding that holding onto resentment and anger ultimately only harms ourselves.

But forgiving others can be a difficult task. It can feel like we are betraying ourselves, like we are condoning the wrong that was done to us. It can feel like we are letting the other person off the hook. But remember, forgiveness is not about them; it's about us. It's about reclaiming our own power, freeing ourselves from the chains of the past.

Take the story of **Sita**, a young woman who had been deeply hurt by a betrayal from a close friend. The pain was so intense, so raw, that it consumed her thoughts, her emotions, and her daily life. She carried this anger and resentment within her, like a heavy stone in her heart.

She tried to move on, but the pain kept pulling her back, reminding her of the betrayal. It affected her relationships, her career, and even her sense of self-worth. She felt like she was constantly fighting against this invisible force, a force fueled by anger and pain.

One day, while attending a yoga retreat, Sita heard a talk about forgiveness. It resonated with her, but she also felt resistant. How could she forgive someone who had hurt her so deeply? She felt like she was betraying herself.

But the speaker's words stayed with her. She realized that she was the one who was truly suffering. She was the one who was carrying the burden of anger and resentment. She realized that by holding onto this pain, she was only hurting herself.

It took time, but Sita eventually started to understand the power of forgiveness. She began to see that forgiving her friend wasn't about condoning her actions, but about freeing herself from the pain that was holding her captive. It was about choosing to release the anger, the bitterness, and the resentment.

The process wasn't easy, but Sita found strength in mindfulness practices and support from her yoga teacher. She learned to let go of the need for revenge, the need to make her friend suffer. She began to understand that her friend was also a human being, flawed and imperfect, just like everyone else.

As Sita slowly began to let go of her anger and resentment, she started to feel a shift within herself. The heaviness in her heart began to lift. She felt lighter, freer. She was finally able to move forward, to embrace new opportunities and build new connections.

Forgiving others is a powerful act of self-love. It's about choosing to let go of the past and moving forward with a lighter heart. But what about forgiving ourselves?

Self-forgiveness is just as important, if not more so, than forgiving others. We all make mistakes. We all have regrets. We all have things we wish we could change. But holding onto these mistakes, dwelling on them, can be a toxic and destructive force.

Imagine a young boy named **Arjun**, a talented artist with a passion for painting. He had dreams of becoming a renowned artist, but his path was filled with obstacles. He faced criticism from his family, who believed that art was a frivolous pursuit. He struggled to find his voice as an artist, and he doubted his abilities.

One day, Arjun had a chance to showcase his work at a prestigious art exhibition. He poured his heart and soul into his paintings, hoping to finally prove his talent. But when the exhibition opened, his work was met with indifference. The critics dismissed his art as amateurish, and the public simply didn't connect with it.

Arjun was devastated. He felt like a failure, a fraud. He blamed himself for his lack of success, believing he wasn't talented enough, that he wasn't worthy of recognition. This failure became a heavy weight he carried with him, hindering his creative drive and dimming his passion for art.

For years, Arjun struggled with self-doubt and guilt. He felt like he had let himself and his family down. He couldn't escape the shadow of his past failure. He distanced himself from his art, fearing another public rejection.

However, as time passed, Arjun began to realize that holding onto this guilt was only harming him. He realized that he had given his best, and that the outcome wasn't a reflection of his worth as an artist. He began to understand that failure is a part of life, a learning opportunity, and not a reflection of his identity.

It wasn't easy, but Arjun began to practice self-compassion. He allowed himself to feel the pain of his past, to acknowledge his mistakes without judging himself harshly. He learned to forgive himself for his failures, recognizing that they were part of his journey.

This process of self-forgiveness was a slow and gradual one. It took time for Arjun to let go of the expectations he had placed on himself, to release the weight of his past failure. But as he learned to forgive himself, he started to feel a shift within him. His creativity was rekindled. His passion for art returned. He began to create again, with a renewed sense of purpose and joy.

Self-forgiveness is an act of radical self-love. It's about recognizing our humanness, acknowledging our mistakes, and choosing to release the guilt and shame that weighs us down. It's about offering ourselves the same grace and understanding that we would offer a loved one.

Forgiveness, whether it's directed at others or at ourselves, is a powerful act of liberation. It's about breaking free from the chains of the past and moving forward with a lighter heart, a more peaceful mind, and a renewed sense of purpose. It's about reclaiming our power and choosing to live a life that is free from the burdens of the past.

As we embark on this journey of forgiveness, it's important to remember that it's not always easy. There will be moments of doubt, moments of anger, moments when we feel like we are back to square one. But it's important to be patient with ourselves, to be compassionate towards our own struggles.

Forgiveness is a process, not an event. It's about taking small steps, releasing the pain bit by bit, until we finally reach a place of peace and acceptance. It's about choosing to be free.

So, let us embrace the power of forgiveness. Let us release the weight of the past, forgive ourselves and others, and step into the freedom that awaits us. Let us choose to live a life that is free from the shackles of resentment, anger, and guilt. Let us choose to live a life filled with love, compassion, and joy.

Forgiving Others

Forgiving others is a powerful act of self-liberation, a key to unlocking happiness and peace within. It's not about condoning the actions of those who have hurt us, but about releasing the grip of resentment and anger that weighs us down. While it may seem impossible at first, especially when the pain feels fresh, forgiveness is a journey, a step-by-step process that leads to healing and freedom.

Imagine a heavy stone, a burden we carry around, representing the bitterness and resentment towards someone who has wronged us. It's a heavy weight, a constant reminder of the pain inflicted, causing discomfort and preventing us from moving forward. Forgiveness is like gently placing that stone down, letting go of its grip and allowing ourselves to find lightness and peace.

Forgiving others is not a sign of weakness; it's an act of strength. It takes courage to confront the pain, acknowledge the hurt, and choose to let go of the negative energy that consumes us. This act of letting go is not for the benefit of the person who wronged us, but for our own well-being. It allows us to break free from the shackles of the past, allowing us to step into a brighter future.

Here are some steps to embark on this journey of forgiveness:

1. Acknowledging the Pain:

The first step towards forgiveness is acknowledging the pain. It's important to validate our emotions, to allow ourselves to feel the hurt and anger, rather than suppressing or denying them. This is a crucial step in the healing process, acknowledging the injustice and the impact it has had on our lives.

Think of this stage like a wound. You wouldn't ignore a wound, you would clean it, treat it, and allow it to heal. Similarly, acknowledging the pain is like cleaning and treating the emotional wound, allowing it to begin the process of healing.

2. Understanding the Other Perspective:

While it's essential to acknowledge our own pain, it's also beneficial to try and understand the other person's perspective. This doesn't mean excusing their actions, but it can help us to gain a deeper understanding of the situation, perhaps even uncovering mitigating factors.

Imagine you are watching a play, and you see one character acting in a hurtful way. To fully understand the play, you need to understand the character's motivations, their backstory, and what drives their actions. Similarly, to fully understand the situation, we need to try and understand the other person's perspective.

This can be difficult, especially when we feel deeply hurt, but attempting to see things from their point of view can help us to break free from the cycle of anger and resentment.

3. Releasing the Grip of Resentment:

Holding onto resentment is like holding onto a hot coal, with the intention of burning someone else, but ultimately, it's only we who get burned. Resentment is like a heavy weight, a constant source of negativity that weighs us down and prevents us from moving forward.

Imagine the weight of resentment as a bag filled with rocks. Each rock represents a hurtful act, and every day we add more rocks to the bag, making it heavier and harder to carry. Forgiveness is like letting go of the rocks, one by one, until the bag feels lighter and easier to carry.

4. Choosing Compassion:

Forgiveness is not about forgetting the hurt or condoning the actions of the other person. It's about choosing compassion, understanding that everyone makes mistakes and that everyone is struggling in their own way.

Imagine a person walking through a forest, and they accidentally step on a flower. They didn't do it intentionally, but they still caused harm. We could choose to be angry and resentful, or we could choose to be compassionate and understand that it was an accident. Compassion allows us to release the anger and move forward with forgiveness.

5. Embracing Self-Forgiveness:

Forgiving others is often a catalyst for forgiving ourselves. The act of releasing resentment toward another can open the door to self-forgiveness, allowing us to release the burden of past mistakes and failures. It's a powerful realization that we too are worthy of forgiveness, and that we can move forward from our own mistakes.

Think of self-forgiveness as a chance to rewrite our story. We've all made mistakes, but those mistakes don't define us. We can choose to learn from them, grow from them, and move forward with a renewed sense of self-acceptance.

6. Practical Steps to Forgiveness:

While the path to forgiveness is a personal journey, there are some practical steps that can aid in the process:

Journaling: Writing about our feelings, the hurt, and the reasons behind our anger can be cathartic, allowing us to process our emotions in a healthy way.

Meditation: Mindfulness and meditation can help us to release the grip of negativity and develop a more compassionate perspective.

Visualization: Imagine releasing the burden of resentment, visualizing the other person in a positive light, or even sending them well wishes.

Talking to Someone: Speaking to a trusted friend, family member, or therapist can provide support and guidance as we navigate the process.

Forgiving Others: A Journey of Transformation

Forgiving others is a journey, a process that takes time and effort. It may not happen overnight, and there may be moments of setbacks and regressions. But with patience, persistence, and self-compassion, it is possible to release the burden of resentment and embrace the freedom of forgiveness.

The journey to forgiveness is a journey of transformation, a journey that leads to healing, peace, and self-liberation. It's an act of strength, a commitment to our own well-being, and a gift we give ourselves to live a life free from the shackles of the past.

Cultural Perspective: The Power of Forgiveness in Indian Culture

Forgiveness holds a profound significance in Indian culture, deeply rooted in its spiritual and philosophical traditions. The concept of **"karma"**, the law of cause and effect, highlights the importance of releasing negative emotions like anger and resentment, as they can perpetuate a cycle of suffering.

Indian philosophy also emphasizes the power of **"ahimsa,"** non-violence, which extends beyond physical harm to include verbal and mental abuse. Forgiveness aligns with this principle, fostering peace and harmony within ourselves and in our interactions with others.

Many ancient Indian texts, such as the **Bhagavad Gita**, emphasize the transformative power of forgiveness. The Gita, a timeless guide to spiritual living, encourages the release of anger, hatred, and resentment, urging individuals to cultivate compassion and forgiveness for their own well-being and the well-being of the world.

Forgiveness: A Gift to Ourselves

Forgiving others is not about forgetting the past; it's about releasing the grip of its negative influences. It's a choice we make, a conscious decision to free ourselves from the burdens of resentment and anger, and to open our hearts to a brighter future.

By embracing the path of forgiveness, we not only liberate ourselves from the chains of the past but also pave the way for greater peace and happiness in our present and future. It's a gift we give ourselves, a gift of freedom, and a gift that allows us to live fully in the present moment, unburdened by the weight of yesterday.

Self Forgiveness

Self-forgiveness is a powerful act of self-compassion and release. It's about acknowledging our mistakes, understanding the context of our actions, and choosing to let go of the burden of guilt and shame. In the Indian tradition, forgiveness is often viewed as a journey of inner liberation, a release from the chains of the past that hinder our growth and happiness.

Imagine a young woman named **Mita**, a talented artist from Mumbai, who struggled with self-doubt and a fear of failure. Growing up, her parents had instilled in her a strong sense of responsibility and a deep fear of disappointment. They emphasized academic success, pushing her to pursue a lucrative career in finance, even though her heart yearned for art. Mita eventually succumbed to their pressure, enrolling in a business school against her will.

Years later, Mita found herself working in a corporate world she didn't enjoy. The pressure was immense, and she often felt overwhelmed and lost. She began to compare herself to her successful peers, feeling inadequate and resentful. This sense of inadequacy translated into a constant inner critic that berated her for not fulfilling her parents' expectations. Deep down, she felt a gnawing sense of regret for choosing the path of practicality over her passion.

As Mita navigated this internal turmoil, she stumbled upon an old book on the teachings of **Mahatma Gandhi**. Gandhi's emphasis on truth and self-reflection resonated with Maya, prompting her to examine her own beliefs and actions. It was then that she realized the root of her unhappiness was her self-judgment and lack of forgiveness. She had been holding onto the past, replaying her "mistake" of choosing a path she didn't love, blaming herself for her perceived failures.

This realization was a turning point for Mita. She began practicing self-compassion, recognizing that her choices were made based on the limited perspective she had at the time. She understood that her parents' love and desire for her well-being had, unknowingly, fueled her fear of disappointment. Mita started forgiving herself for following the path they had laid out for her, realizing that she had acted to the best of her knowledge and capability.

One way Mita began to practice self-forgiveness was by writing down her feelings and experiences. She poured her heart onto paper, acknowledging her regrets, her disappointments, and the feelings of shame that had burdened her for so long. Through writing, she started to unpack her emotions, exploring the reasons behind her choices. She even wrote letters to her past self, offering compassion and understanding, reassuring herself that it was okay to make mistakes and that she could always choose a different path.

Mita's journey of self-forgiveness also involved a conscious shift in her perspective. Instead of seeing her past as a series of failures, she started viewing it as a learning experience. She recognized that her corporate experience, while challenging, had equipped her with valuable skills and insights. She discovered that her fear of failure had actually spurred her to develop resilience and resourcefulness. This newfound perspective empowered her to embrace her past experiences, not as burdens, but as steppingstones on her journey toward self-discovery and fulfillment.

Another crucial aspect of Mita's self-forgiveness was actively seeking support. She opened up to her closest friends and family about her internal struggles, sharing her desire to pursue her passion for art. To her surprise, they were incredibly supportive, encouraging her to explore her artistic side and embrace her true self. Their acceptance and encouragement gave her the strength to take the first steps towards her dreams.

Mita eventually decided to quit her corporate job and enroll in an art program. The decision was not without its anxieties, but she was determined to live a life aligned with her passions. The journey wasn't easy, but she learned to navigate the challenges with grace and resilience. She found joy in the creative process, discovering new ways to express herself through art.

As Mita embraced her artistic path, she experienced a profound shift within herself. The weight of self-judgment and regret gradually lifted, replaced by a sense of self-acceptance and contentment. She had forgiven herself for past choices, learned from her experiences, and emerged stronger, more confident, and true to herself.

Mita's story highlights the transformative power of self-forgiveness. It's not about erasing the past or condoning mistakes; it's about freeing ourselves from the chains of guilt and shame that hold us back from living authentically. When we learn to forgive ourselves, we make space for compassion, acceptance, and growth. We open ourselves up to new possibilities and embrace the potential for a fulfilling and meaningful life.

The journey of self-forgiveness can be challenging, but it's a path worth taking. It requires courage, honesty, and a willingness to let go. Like Mita, we can all learn to release the past, embrace the present, and embark on a journey of personal growth and transformation. Forgiving ourselves is a gift we give ourselves, a gift of liberation that allows us to live fully and authentically, embracing the journey of life with openness and joy.

As you embark on your own journey of self-forgiveness, here are some practical steps you can take:

1. Acknowledge Your Mistakes and Emotions:

- Begin by acknowledging your mistakes and the negative emotions associated with them. Don't try to minimize or ignore them. Allow yourself to feel the pain, anger, or shame, but without judgment.

2. Examine Your Past:

- Explore the context of your past actions. What were the circumstances that led to your mistakes? What were your motivations? Were there any external factors that influenced your decisions? Understanding the context can help you gain a more compassionate perspective.

3. Forgive Yourself:

- Once you have acknowledged your mistakes and the reasons behind them, make a conscious decision to forgive yourself. Tell yourself, "I forgive myself for [the mistake]". This act of forgiveness is about releasing the burden of guilt and allowing yourself to move forward.

4. Practice Self-Compassion:

- Treat yourself with the same kindness and understanding you would offer a dear friend. Be patient with yourself, recognizing that everyone makes mistakes.

5. Shift Your Perspective:

- Learn from your past experiences without letting them define you. See your mistakes as opportunities for growth and learning. Remember that every challenge, every setback, offers a chance to learn and evolve.

6. Embrace the Present:

- Focus on the present moment. Living in the present allows you to appreciate the beauty of life and to create a fulfilling future.

7. Seek Support:

- Share your journey with trusted friends, family, or a therapist. Having someone to listen and offer support can be invaluable.

8. Practice Gratitude:

- Focus on the positive aspects of your life, expressing gratitude for the people and experiences that bring you joy.

9. Engage in Meaningful Activities:

- Pursue activities that align with your values and passions. Engaging in meaningful work, hobbies, or relationships can bring a sense of purpose and fulfillment.

10. Visualize Your Future:

- Imagine a future filled with peace, joy, and self-acceptance. Visualizing a positive future can help you cultivate a hopeful and optimistic mindset.

The journey of self-forgiveness is a lifelong process, a continuous practice of releasing the past and embracing the present. It's a journey of self-discovery, self-compassion, and growth. As you move forward, remember that forgiveness is a powerful act of love and self-care, a gift you give yourself to live a life filled with joy, purpose, and peace.

The Freedom of Letting Go

Forgiveness, like a gentle breeze, whispers through the tangled branches of our past, offering release from the heavy weight of resentment and hurt. It is a delicate dance of letting go, a conscious choice to unburden ourselves from the chains of anger and bitterness that bind us to the past.

Imagine a young woman named **Usha**, her heart heavy with the weight of a past betrayal. Years ago, her best friend, Rita, had broken a promise, leaving Usha feeling abandoned and hurt. The memory of that betrayal had become a constant shadow, casting a pall over Usha's present joy. Every time Rita's name crossed her lips, a wave of anger and bitterness would surge through her.

Usha found herself caught in a vicious cycle. She couldn't forgive Rita, yet she couldn't let go of the pain either. The anger gnawed at her, stealing her peace of mind and preventing her from forming new connections. She realized that the anger wasn't just hurting Rita, it was also hurting her, holding her captive in the prison of her own past.

The turning point came when Usha stumbled upon an ancient Indian proverb: *"Holding onto anger is like grasping a hot coal with the intent of throwing it at someone else; you are the one who gets burned."* This proverb struck a chord deep within Usha, illuminating the truth of her own experience. She realized that the anger she was holding onto was burning her, not Rita.

Driven by a yearning for freedom, Usha embarked on a journey of forgiveness. It wasn't easy. There were moments of doubt, moments where the pain felt overwhelming. But she reminded herself of the proverb's wisdom, the truth that holding onto anger was ultimately hurting her more than anyone else.

One sunny afternoon, Usha decided to confront Rita. Instead of lashing out with anger, she spoke from the heart, expressing the pain she had carried for years. Rita listened with genuine remorse, acknowledging the hurt she had caused. In that moment of honesty and vulnerability, a healing began to take place.

Usha realized that forgiveness wasn't about condoning Rita's actions, nor was it about forgetting the hurt. It was about choosing to release the anger and bitterness that had been poisoning her soul. It was about taking back her power, choosing to let go of the past and embrace the freedom that lay ahead.

Forgiveness, like a gentle rain, washed away the residue of bitterness, leaving behind a sense of lightness and peace. Priya felt a new wave of energy coursing through her, a newfound ability to connect with others without the weight of the past holding her back.

This journey of forgiveness was not just about Usha and Rita. It was a testament to the power of forgiveness to heal old wounds, to break free from the chains of the past, and to reclaim our own peace of mind.

Forgiveness is not a sign of weakness, but a testament to our strength. It is the courage to let go of the anger, resentment, and pain that hold us captive. It is the willingness to release ourselves from the burden of the past, to choose healing over bitterness, and to open ourselves to the possibility of a brighter future.

Forgiveness is a transformative act, a journey of self-discovery and liberation. It is a choice we make, a conscious decision to release ourselves from the shackles of the past and embrace the freedom of the present.

Let us learn from Usha's journey, embrace the wisdom of forgiveness, and embark on our own path to liberation. Let us choose to release the anger and bitterness that hold us captive, and step into the light of a future free from the chains of the past.

Now, let's consider the concept of self-forgiveness. While forgiving others can be a challenging but rewarding process, forgiving ourselves for past mistakes can be even more daunting. We often judge ourselves harshly, replaying our missteps on a mental loop, convinced that we are not worthy of forgiveness.

Imagine a young man named **Raj**, struggling with the aftermath of a failed business venture. He had poured his heart and soul into the project, only to watch it crumble before his eyes. The failure had left him feeling ashamed, incompetent, and unworthy. The voice of self-doubt echoed in his mind, reminding him of his shortcomings.

Raj found himself trapped in a cycle of self-blame. He couldn't forgive himself for his mistakes, for his inability to foresee the pitfalls that ultimately led to the business' downfall. He constantly replayed the scenarios in his mind, wishing he could rewind time and make different choices.

This relentless self-criticism prevented Raj from moving forward. It stifled his creativity, hampered his confidence, and left him feeling stuck in a rut of self-doubt. He felt like a failure, incapable of achieving his dreams.

The turning point came when Raj came across an ancient Indian scripture, the **Bhagavad Gita**, which emphasized the importance of self-acceptance and forgiveness. It reminded him that everyone makes mistakes, that failures are inevitable parts of life, and that true strength lies in learning from our mistakes and moving forward.

Inspired by the scripture's wisdom, Raj began to practice self-compassion. He acknowledged his mistakes, but he also recognized his strengths and the lessons he had learned from the experience. He started to view the failure not as a sign of his inadequacy, but as an opportunity for growth.

Gradually, Raj began to forgive himself. He released the weight of self-blame and replaced it with self-acceptance. He realized that his mistakes did not define him, and that he had the power to learn from them and build a better future.

Raj's journey taught him that true forgiveness is not about erasing the past or denying our mistakes. It is about acknowledging our shortcomings, accepting responsibility for our actions, and choosing to move forward with compassion and grace.

Self-forgiveness is a crucial step on the path to liberation. It allows us to break free from the chains of self-judgment and to embrace the possibility of a brighter future. It is about understanding that our mistakes are not a reflection of our worth, but simply part of our human experience.

Like a gentle rain that nourishes the earth, self-forgiveness nourishes our soul, allowing us to grow and blossom. It is the key to unlocking our potential and to living a life filled with purpose and joy.

As we delve deeper into the realm of forgiveness, we must also acknowledge the role of time. Forgiveness is not a quick fix, but rather a gradual process that unfolds over time. It is a journey that requires patience, compassion, and unwavering commitment to self-growth.

Think of forgiveness as a river, flowing gently through the landscape of our lives. Sometimes the river encounters obstacles, rocks, and fallen logs, creating ripples and eddies. These obstacles represent the hurts, betrayals, and mistakes that we encounter along the way.

Just as the river navigates these obstacles, we too can navigate the challenges of forgiveness. It might take time for the anger and resentment to subside, for the wounds to heal, for the river to smooth its flow. But with patience, compassion, and a willingness to let go, the river of forgiveness will eventually find its way to calmer waters.

Time plays a crucial role in this process. It allows us to gain perspective, to see the situation from a broader vantage point, and to understand the complexities of human nature. It allows us to release the grip of our emotions and to embrace a more rational and compassionate approach to forgiveness.

Remember, forgiveness is not a sign of weakness, but a testament to our strength. It is about choosing to let go, to release ourselves from the burden of the past, and to embrace the possibility of a brighter future.

Embrace the power of time. Allow yourself the space and grace to heal. Trust that the journey of forgiveness is a process, and that with patience and compassion, you will find your way to a place of peace and liberation.

Forgiveness is a gift we give ourselves. It is a choice to release the anger and bitterness that hold us captive, to choose healing over resentment, and to open ourselves to the possibilities of a brighter future.

Now, let's explore how forgiveness can free us from emotional pain.

Emotional pain is an integral part of the human experience. It arises from loss, hurt, betrayal, and the myriad challenges we face throughout our lives. While some pain may be fleeting, certain experiences can leave lasting scars, creating emotional wounds that can fester and affect our well-being.

These emotional wounds can manifest in various ways, such as feelings of anger, resentment, sadness, guilt, shame, or anxiety. They can disrupt our relationships, impact our self-esteem, and prevent us from living our lives to the fullest.

Think of emotional pain as a heavy weight, a burden we carry with us, a reminder of the hurt we have experienced. This weight can be debilitating, affecting our physical and mental health, our relationships, and our overall sense of well-being.

Just as a heavy weight can make it difficult to move forward, so too can emotional pain hinder our progress. It can prevent us from forming new connections, embracing opportunities, and experiencing true joy.

Forgiveness, like a gentle hand, can help us release the weight of emotional pain. It is the key to unlocking the freedom and peace that lie beyond the confines of our hurt.

Consider the story of a young woman named **Reena**. She had been in a long-term relationship that ended abruptly and painfully. The betrayal she experienced left deep emotional wounds, causing her to withdraw from others and to doubt her own worthiness.

Reena carried the pain of the broken relationship with her, replaying the events in her mind, reliving the hurt, and blaming herself for what had happened. The emotional weight she carried prevented her from forming new connections and from experiencing true joy.

But then, Reena discovered the power of forgiveness. She recognized that holding onto the pain was only hurting her, that it was preventing her from moving forward. She decided to embark on a journey of forgiveness, not just for her ex-partner, but for herself as well.

The journey was not easy. There were moments of tears, moments of anger, and moments of doubt. But Reena persevered, reminding herself of the importance of forgiveness.

With time and effort, Reena began to release the weight of her emotional pain. She forgave her ex-partner for his actions, understanding that he was not responsible for her happiness. She forgave herself for the choices she had made, recognizing that she was not defined by her past.

The act of forgiveness allowed Reena to reclaim her sense of self-worth and to open herself to new possibilities. It freed her from the chains of the past and allowed her to step into the light of a brighter future.

Reena's story highlights the transformative power of forgiveness. It demonstrates how releasing the weight of emotional pain can unlock true freedom, allowing us to experience peace, joy, and fulfillment.

Forgiveness is not about forgetting the past or condoning wrongdoings. It is about choosing to let go of the anger, resentment, and bitterness that hold us captive. It is about releasing the weight of emotional pain and reclaiming our peace of mind.

Forgiveness is a powerful tool for healing and liberation. It is the key to unlocking the freedom and joy that lie beyond the confines of our hurt. Embrace the power of forgiveness, and allow it to set you free from the emotional chains that bind you to the past.

The journey of forgiveness can be a transformative experience, a journey of self-discovery and liberation. It is a process that requires courage, patience, and unwavering commitment. But the rewards are immense. By choosing to forgive, we choose to release the weight of emotional pain, to reclaim our power, and to step into the light of a brighter future.

The Indian philosopher and poet, **Kabir**, wrote: *"If you want to live a happy life, tie it to a goal, not to people or things."* This wisdom applies not only to our goals but also to our emotional well-being. When we tie our happiness to the actions of others, we become vulnerable to their choices and susceptible to emotional pain. But when we choose to forgive, we untie ourselves from the expectations and resentments that bind us to the past.

Forgiveness is a gift we give ourselves, a gift of freedom, a gift of peace. It is a choice we make every day, a choice to let go of the past and embrace the possibility of a brighter future.

As we embark on our journey of forgiveness, let us remember the words of the ancient Indian sage, **Lao Tzu:** *"Being deeply loved by someone gives you strength, while loving someone deeply gives you courage."* The courage to forgive, to release the pain and to embrace the present moment is a testament to our strength and a source of deep inner peace.

Forgiveness is a journey of liberation, a path that leads us to a place of peace, joy, and fulfillment. Let us choose to walk this path, one step at a time, and embrace the transformative power of forgiveness.

<u>Personal Forgiveness Journey</u>

Forgiveness is a powerful act of liberation, a choice to release ourselves from the chains of bitterness and resentment. It's not about condoning wrongdoing; it's about breaking free from the emotional prison that keeps us tethered to the past. It's about finding the strength to let go of the anger, hurt, and pain that we hold onto, often without realizing the weight it carries.

Forgiving others can be a daunting task, especially when the wounds run deep. It demands courage, empathy, and a willingness to understand the complexities of human nature. But the journey toward forgiveness is not about erasing the past; it's about choosing to move beyond it. It's about recognizing that holding onto anger and resentment only serves to poison our own hearts, preventing us from experiencing true peace and joy.

Imagine a tapestry woven with threads of vibrant colors, each representing a memory, an experience, a relationship. Some threads are bright and beautiful, reflecting joyful moments and cherished connections. Others are dark and heavy, carrying the weight of hurt, betrayal, and loss. The threads of the past, both good and bad, make up the tapestry of our lives. But clinging to the dark threads, holding on to the pain, can cause the tapestry to become frayed and distorted, obscuring the beauty of the brighter threads.

Forgiveness, in this context, is about choosing to let go of those dark threads. It's about releasing the hold of past experiences that continue to cast a shadow over our present. It's about gently unwinding the knots of bitterness and resentment, allowing ourselves to see the tapestry of our lives in a new light.

But forgiveness isn't just about others; it's also about ourselves. We all make mistakes, and sometimes, our actions can cause hurt to ourselves and those around us. Self-forgiveness can be the most challenging form of forgiveness, as it requires us to confront our own flaws and imperfections. Yet, it's essential for our well-being and growth.

Imagine a young woman named **Amrita**, a talented musician who had always dreamed of performing on a grand stage. After years of practice and dedication, she finally landed an audition for a prestigious music festival. Filled with excitement and anticipation, she poured her heart and soul into the performance, giving it her all. But despite her best efforts, she didn't get selected.

The disappointment hit her like a wave, washing over her with a crushing force. She blamed herself for her shortcomings, her inadequacies, the weight of her past failures. She felt like a failure, unworthy of her dreams, trapped in a cycle of self-doubt and self-criticism.

The sting of rejection lingered, casting a shadow over her passion and her spirit. For months, Amrita struggled to find her way back to music, her love for it dimmed by the pain of her failure. Her friends, sensing her distress, encouraged her to pursue her dream, but she couldn't shake the feeling of inadequacy.

One day, as Amrita sat by the river, watching the water flow calmly, a profound realization dawned upon her. She realized that her pursuit of perfection had become a prison, a barrier to her own growth. She had allowed the fear of failure to overshadow her love for music, and in the process, she had lost sight of her own journey.

That day, Amrita decided to let go of the past. She acknowledged her disappointment but refused to let it define her. She recognized that her passion for music had not diminished; it was simply overshadowed by her fear. She began to forgive herself, not for her mistakes, but for the harsh judgment she had imposed upon herself.

Amrita slowly started to reconnect with her love for music, practicing with a renewed sense of purpose. She began to see her journey not as a series of failures, but as a series of lessons learned, experiences that had shaped her into the musician she was becoming.

She realized that true growth comes not from avoiding mistakes, but from learning from them. It comes from embracing our imperfections, from accepting that we are not perfect, but that we are constantly evolving.

With a newfound sense of freedom and self-acceptance, Amrita approached her music with a fresh perspective. She started performing at local events, sharing her passion with a wider audience. Gradually, her confidence returned, and she began to receive positive feedback and recognition for her talent.

Amrita's journey is a testament to the transformative power of self-forgiveness. It's a reminder that we are all on a journey of growth and that we can choose to let go of the past and embrace the future with open arms.

There are countless stories of individuals who have embraced forgiveness and found freedom on the other side. A man named Rahul, haunted by a childhood filled with neglect and abuse, found himself struggling to form healthy relationships. He carried the weight of the past, fearing rejection and abandonment. But through therapy and the guidance of a supportive community, he began to understand that the past was not his present. He learned to forgive himself and his abusers, allowing him to break free from the cycle of pain and find healing.

A woman named **Hema**, a successful entrepreneur, faced a devastating business setback that shattered her confidence and threatened to derail her career. She blamed herself for the failure, dwelling on her mistakes and questioning her abilities. But with the support of her family and friends, she realized that failure was not the end. She found the strength to forgive herself, to learn from her mistakes, and to rebuild her business with renewed determination.

These stories are a testament to the resilience of the human spirit, our capacity for growth and transformation. Forgiveness is not a sign of weakness; it's a sign of strength, a willingness to let go of the past and embrace the present. It's about recognizing that holding onto anger and resentment only harms us, while forgiveness opens the door to healing, peace, and freedom.

As we embark on our own journeys of forgiveness, we must be patient with ourselves. The process of forgiveness can be challenging, often requiring us to confront difficult emotions and memories. But with each step we take, with each moment of compassion and understanding, we move closer to liberation.

Forgiveness is a gift we give ourselves, a gift that unlocks the potential for a brighter, more fulfilling future. It's a gift that allows us to break free from the shackles of the past and step into the light of the present moment.

5

REWRITING YOUR NARRATIVE

The Power of Perspective

The power of perspective is like a magic lens that can shift the focus of our story, highlighting different details and altering the overall narrative. Just as a painter can use light and shadow to create depth and emotion, we can use perspective to rewrite our life stories, transforming them from tales of hardship into chronicles of growth and resilience.

Imagine a family gathering, where a particular relative always brings up a past mistake – a missed opportunity, a hurtful word, or a moment of failure. They relive the event, rehashing the details, and letting the shadow of that incident darken the present celebration. This is the trap of a fixed perspective – clinging to a single point of view, refusing to acknowledge the broader landscape of experience.

But what if, instead of dwelling on the mistake, the relative focused on the lessons learned? What if they acknowledged the courage it took to try something new, the resilience demonstrated in facing the consequences, and the wisdom gained from the experience? The narrative shifts, transforming from one of defeat to one of resilience and growth. This, in essence, is the power of perspective.

Our lives are filled with such moments – missed opportunities, hurtful words, and failures that feel like indelible stains on our narrative. But these experiences need not define us. We have the power to choose a different perspective, to look at the same event through a lens of learning, growth, and even gratitude.

For instance, consider a woman who felt she had wasted her youth chasing a career that ultimately didn't fulfill her. She might be consumed by the regret of lost time, the missed opportunities for personal growth, and the feeling of starting over at a later age. Her narrative could be one of lost potential and missed chances. But what if she shifted her perspective? What if she acknowledged that her career, despite not being her dream, had provided invaluable life lessons, built resilience, and equipped her with skills and knowledge she wouldn't have otherwise acquired? What if she saw her current situation as an opportunity for a fresh start, to pursue passions she had long ignored? By changing her perspective, she could transform her narrative from one of regret into one of second chances and newfound purpose.

This power of perspective extends beyond personal experiences. It can also transform our perception of challenging situations, external obstacles, and even our own limitations.

Think of a student struggling with a particular subject in school. Their perspective might be focused on their perceived lack of ability, the frustration of repeated failures, and the looming pressure of exams. This perspective might lead to feelings of inadequacy, fear of further setbacks, and a reluctance to engage with the subject further. However, if they shift their perspective, they might see the struggle as an opportunity for growth. They might see the challenge as a chance to develop resilience, to learn new strategies, and to discover a different approach. By viewing the obstacle as a learning experience, they might find a renewed sense of motivation, a deeper understanding of the subject, and a greater appreciation for the journey of overcoming obstacles.

The Indian philosophy of **"karma yoga"** offers a valuable lens for understanding this power of perspective. Karma yoga emphasizes action without attachment to the outcome. It teaches us to focus on the present moment, on performing our duties with dedication and mindfulness, without dwelling on past successes or failures. This approach can help us detach from the limiting perspectives of self-judgment and regret, allowing us to embrace the present moment and focus on the journey of growth and transformation.

The key to shifting perspective is to develop a conscious awareness of our thoughts and emotions. This means regularly pausing to examine our inner dialogue, noticing when we are replaying negative experiences, and actively challenging those limiting thoughts. It means seeking out positive interpretations, finding the silver linings, and acknowledging the lessons learned, even from seemingly negative experiences.

It is also essential to cultivate gratitude, to focus on the blessings in our lives, and to appreciate the good things that exist, even amidst challenges. Gratitude can shift our perspective from a scarcity mindset to one of abundance, allowing us to see the richness and beauty that often goes unnoticed when we are fixated on the negative.

The ability to shift perspective is a skill that can be cultivated. It requires practice and conscious effort, but the rewards are immense. By rewriting our narratives, by choosing to see challenges as opportunities, and by embracing a more positive and empowering perspective, we unlock the potential for personal growth, resilience, and fulfillment. We begin to write a new chapter in our life story, one that is filled with hope, possibility, and the transformative power of living fully in the present moment.

Crafting a New Story

The past holds a captivating power. It whispers stories of joy, sorrow, triumph, and defeat, weaving itself into the very fabric of our being. It shapes our perceptions, influences our decisions, and colors our present moments. Yet, while the past is undeniably a part of who we are, its grip can become a prison if we allow it to define our future.

In this chapter, we embark on a journey of self-discovery, not to deny the past, but to understand its influence and reclaim our narrative. The goal is not to erase the past, but to rewrite it, transforming its power from a shackle to a steppingstone.

Imagine a canvas, pristine white and full of potential. As we navigate life, each experience, each interaction, adds a brushstroke to this canvas. Some strokes are vibrant, filled with the colors of joy and success. Others are somber, painted in shades of loss, regret, and pain. The canvas becomes a tapestry, reflecting the rich tapestry of our lives.

However, sometimes, we become fixated on specific strokes, clinging to them with an almost desperate intensity. We dwell on past triumphs, reliving the golden moments, but also forgetting the accompanying struggles. We become tethered to past failures, replaying the missteps in our minds, allowing them to define our self-worth. This relentless focus on the past can lead to a sense of stagnation, trapping us in a cycle of what could have been, what should have been, or what we believe we are destined to repeat.

In the Indian tradition, we find a beautiful metaphor for this. Imagine a **"karmic"** rope, a weighty thread woven from the actions, thoughts, and emotions of our past. This rope binds us to our past, influencing our present and shaping our future. But, within this tradition, there is also a powerful belief in "karma yoga," the path of selfless action. It suggests that by focusing on the present, by performing our duties with dedication and without attachment to the outcomes, we can begin to loosen the grip of the karmic rope, freeing ourselves from the shackles of the past.

This is the essence of rewriting our narrative. It's about recognizing the power of the past while simultaneously choosing to break free from its constraints. It's about acknowledging the lessons learned but choosing to move forward with a sense of possibility and hope.

So, how do we rewrite our narratives? How do we transform the past from a burden to a springboard for growth? This is where the art of perspective comes in.

Imagine a single, powerful stroke of red on our canvas. If we zoom in, we might see only its intensity, its dominance. But, if we step back and view the canvas as a whole, we see that this red stroke is just one small element in a larger composition. It's part of a vibrant tapestry, contributing to the overall beauty and depth of the artwork.

Rewriting our narrative involves taking this step back, viewing our lives from a broader perspective. We acknowledge the impact of past experiences, the joy, the sorrow, the triumphs, and the setbacks. But, we also recognize that these are but threads in the intricate tapestry of our lives. They are part of our story, but not the entire story.

This perspective shift is the foundation for crafting a new story, a narrative that empowers us to live fully in the present and create a future that we desire. It's about letting go of the grip of the past and embracing the possibilities of the present.

The journey of rewriting our narratives begins with acknowledging our past, its strengths, and its weaknesses. We need to understand how it has shaped us, what lessons it holds, and how it might be influencing our current actions and choices. But, this journey also involves actively embracing the power of the present moment.

This is where mindfulness comes in. Mindfulness, as we explored in the previous chapter, is the practice of paying attention to the present moment without judgment. It's about tuning into our thoughts, feelings, and sensations, acknowledging them without getting caught up in them. This practice allows us to step away from the relentless cycle of past memories and future anxieties, grounding us in the present.

Through mindfulness, we can observe our thoughts about the past, noticing how they might be affecting our emotions and behavior. We can cultivate a sense of detachment from these thoughts, allowing them to pass through our awareness without clinging to them. This detachment creates space for new possibilities, new perspectives, and a renewed sense of hope.

Rewriting our narratives also involves a profound act of self-forgiveness. We all make mistakes, stumble, and fall. We hold onto regrets, replaying past missteps in our minds, beating ourselves up for things we can't change. This self-criticism can be a heavy burden, weighing us down and hindering our ability to move forward.

Forgiveness, as we saw in the previous chapter, is not about condoning past actions. It's about releasing the grip of resentment and anger, both towards ourselves and others. It's about recognizing that we are all human, capable of both great things and terrible mistakes.

Self-forgiveness is a powerful act of compassion, a recognition of our inherent humanity. It's about acknowledging our mistakes, learning from them, and choosing to move forward with grace and understanding. It's about choosing to believe that we are worthy of love, acceptance, and happiness, despite our past imperfections.

Once we have embraced forgiveness, we can begin to create a new story, a narrative that reflects our present aspirations and future goals. It's about envisioning the life we want to live, the person we want to become, and taking the first steps towards making that vision a reality.

This process of rewriting our narratives is not a linear journey. It's a continuous process of self-discovery, growth, and transformation. We will encounter setbacks, make mistakes, and face challenges along the way. But, each setback becomes an opportunity for learning, each mistake a chance for growth, and each challenge a catalyst for resilience.

Remember, rewriting our narratives is not about erasing the past. It's about recognizing its influence while simultaneously choosing to live authentically in the present. It's about embracing the power of perspective, cultivating mindfulness, practicing forgiveness, and creating a new story that empowers us to live a life of purpose, joy, and fulfillment.

The past holds a powerful grip, but we have the power to break free from its shackles. We have the power to rewrite our stories, create a new narrative, and embrace a future filled with possibility.

This is the journey we embark on in the chapters to come. We will explore how to embrace change, set new goals, build resilience, and navigate the complexities of cultural expectations. We will delve into the transformative power of gratitude and the profound impact of living fully in the present.

Let us begin this journey together. Let us rewrite our narratives, one step, one breath, one moment at a time.

Embracing Change

Change is an inevitable and essential aspect of life. It's the constant hum beneath the surface of our existence, the driving force behind growth, evolution, and personal transformation. Yet, for many of us, change can be a source of fear, anxiety, and resistance. We cling to the familiarity of the past, afraid to let go of what we know, even if it no longer serves us.

Imagine a majestic banyan tree, its roots deeply embedded in the earth, its branches reaching towards the sky, a symbol of steadfastness and enduring strength. This tree, however, is also a testament to the power of adaptation. As the seasons change, its leaves shift colors, falling and giving way to new growth. This cycle of renewal is a constant reminder that change is not an enemy to be fought but a natural rhythm of life.

In the same way, our lives are in a constant state of flux. Just as the seasons shift from winter's slumber to spring's awakening, our own journeys are marked by transitions, both big and small. We graduate from school, enter the workforce, navigate the challenges of relationships, face losses and setbacks, and experience moments of triumph and joy. Each of these experiences shapes us, leaves its mark on our hearts, and contributes to the tapestry of our lives.

However, it's in our human nature to resist change, to hold onto the comfort of the familiar. We crave certainty, predictability, and the sense of control that comes from knowing what to expect. Change, on the other hand, brings uncertainty, challenges us to adapt, and pushes us outside our comfort zones.

Think of a river winding its way through the landscape. Its course is constantly evolving, guided by the flow of water, the erosion of the banks, and the changing seasons. Some stretches are calm and predictable, while others are turbulent and challenging. Yet, the river continues to flow, adapting to its surroundings, carving out new pathways, and ultimately reaching its destination.

Our lives, too, are like a river, ever-changing and evolving. Just as the river doesn't resist the flow of water, but rather navigates it, we, too, must learn to embrace change as a natural part of our journey. Resisting change only creates resistance within ourselves, hindering our growth and preventing us from reaching our full potential.

Imagine a potter shaping clay on a wheel. The clay, initially formless, is transformed into a beautiful vessel through the constant movement of the potter's hands. The potter doesn't fight the clay's resistance, but instead, works with it, guiding it, shaping it, and allowing it to take form.

In the same way, we must learn to work with the changes in our lives, not against them. Change is not something to be feared, but rather an opportunity for growth, transformation, and a deeper understanding of ourselves.

The key lies in shifting our perspective, recognizing change as an inevitable part of life, and learning to navigate it with grace and acceptance. It's not about denying our feelings of fear or resistance, but rather acknowledging them, allowing them to pass, and then moving forward with courage and curiosity.

Embracing change begins with cultivating a sense of openness to new experiences, challenges, and opportunities. It means being willing to step outside our comfort zones, to explore new paths, and to embrace the unknown. It's about trusting that even though change can be unsettling, it ultimately leads to growth, resilience, and a richer, more fulfilling life.

Just as a caterpillar transforms into a butterfly, we too are capable of incredible transformations. It's through embracing change, navigating its challenges, and learning from its lessons that we unlock our true potential and create a life that is both meaningful and authentic.

<u>Here are some practical tips for embracing change:</u>

Cultivate a Growth Mindset: Approach change with a mindset of learning and growth, rather than fear or resistance. See challenges as opportunities for learning and expanding your horizons.

Embrace the Unknown: Instead of fearing the unknown, view it as a chance for adventure and discovery. Step outside your comfort zone and explore new possibilities.

Focus on the Present: Rather than dwelling on the past or worrying about the future, focus your attention on the present moment. Embrace the beauty and possibilities of each day.

Practice Mindfulness: Mindfulness techniques can help you become more aware of your thoughts, emotions, and bodily sensations, allowing you to navigate change with greater clarity and acceptance.

Seek Support: Surround yourself with positive and supportive individuals who can offer encouragement and guidance during times of change.

Celebrate Small Victories: Acknowledge and celebrate your progress, no matter how small it may seem. This helps build confidence and reinforces your ability to adapt and thrive in the face of change.

Remember, change is a constant companion on our journey of life. By embracing it as a natural and necessary part of our growth, we can create a life that is both meaningful and fulfilling. We can learn to navigate the currents of change with grace and resilience, and emerge stronger and wiser on the other side.

Setting New Goals

The past is a powerful teacher, but it can also become a prison. It can hold us back from achieving our full potential if we allow it to define us. Rewriting your narrative is about taking control of your story, embracing a fresh perspective, and charting a course for a future filled with purpose and meaning. This journey involves recognizing the limitations that past experiences have placed on you, and then actively choosing to break free from those constraints.

Imagine a tapestry woven with threads of different colors and textures. Each thread represents an event, a feeling, a relationship from your past. Some threads are vibrant and joyous, while others are dark and painful. As we weave through life, we often carry the weight of every thread, allowing them to dictate the shape and direction of our tapestry.

But what if we could choose which threads to embrace and which ones to let go of? What if we could consciously choose to create a new tapestry, one that reflects our current desires and aspirations, our newfound understanding of who we are and what we want to achieve?

Rewriting your narrative is about consciously choosing to create a new tapestry, one that reflects your current desires and aspirations, your newfound understanding of who you are and what you want to achieve. It's about shifting your perspective, shedding the weight of limiting beliefs, and embracing a future filled with possibilities.

The first step in rewriting your narrative is understanding the power of your own perspective. Our perspective shapes our reality. It determines how we interpret events, how we perceive the world, and how we ultimately shape our future. Sometimes our perspective becomes ingrained, forming a fixed lens through which we view the world. This fixed lens can be a product of past experiences, cultural influences, or simply the way we've always seen things. But just as a photographer can change the lens on their camera to capture a different view, we can also choose to shift our perspective.

Imagine two people looking at the same sunset. One person sees the beauty of the sky, the vibrant colors, the way the light dances on the horizon. The other person sees only the darkness, the fading light, the end of the day. Both are experiencing the same event, but their perspectives are vastly different. This is the power of perspective. It influences how we experience the world and the choices we make.

To rewrite your narrative, you must start by challenging your limiting beliefs. These are the negative thoughts and assumptions that hold you back, whispering doubts and fears that prevent you from reaching your full potential. These beliefs might be rooted in past failures, negative experiences, or even the expectations of others. They might tell you that you're not good enough, that you're not capable of achieving your dreams, or that you're destined to repeat the mistakes of your past.

But remember, these beliefs are just stories we tell ourselves. They are not truths etched in stone. We have the power to challenge these beliefs and rewrite the narrative of our lives. To do this, we need to become conscious of the limiting beliefs that hold us captive. Ask yourself, what are the stories I tell myself? What negative thoughts keep me from reaching my goals? Once you identify these limiting beliefs, you can begin to challenge them.

Think about the stories you tell yourself. Are they based on facts or on assumptions? Do they serve you or hold you back? For example, if you believe you are not good enough, ask yourself: What evidence supports this belief? Have you always been unsuccessful, or are there examples where you have achieved success? Can you identify any negative experiences that have shaped this belief? By examining the basis of your beliefs, you can begin to question their validity.

Rewriting your narrative is a process of continual self-reflection and growth. It's about consciously choosing to embrace a more positive and empowering perspective. It's about shifting your mindset from one of fear and doubt to one of courage and optimism. It's about acknowledging your past but choosing to create a future that is aligned with your deepest values and aspirations.

One powerful technique for rewriting your narrative is to focus on your strengths. We often dwell on our weaknesses, our failures, and our limitations. This can create a sense of negativity and self-doubt. But by focusing on our strengths, we can shift our perspective and create a more positive and empowered sense of self.

Think about your skills, your talents, your unique abilities. What are you good at? What do you enjoy doing? What brings you a sense of fulfillment? Make a list of your strengths and celebrate them. Embrace the qualities that make you special. These strengths are the building blocks of your future.

Rewriting your narrative also involves setting new goals. Goals are like compass points, guiding us towards our desired future. When we set clear and specific goals, we give ourselves a sense of direction and purpose. We create a vision for our lives that we can strive to achieve.

But goal setting is more than just making a list. It's about identifying what truly matters to you, what brings you joy, and what aligns with your deepest values. Goals should be inspiring and challenging, but they should also be attainable. If your goals feel overwhelming, break them down into smaller, more manageable steps. This will make them feel less daunting and more achievable.

As you set new goals, it's important to be honest with yourself about what you truly desire. Don't let societal expectations, family pressures, or your own limiting beliefs dictate your goals. Connect with your deepest desires and aspirations. What truly makes your heart sing? What brings you a sense of purpose and fulfillment?

When you set goals that are aligned with your values, you're more likely to stay motivated and committed to achieving them. You're creating a future that is authentically yours, a future that reflects who you are and what you want to become.

Remember, the process of rewriting your narrative is ongoing. It's a journey of self-discovery and continuous growth. There will be moments of doubt, challenges, and setbacks. But with each step you take, with each goal you achieve, you're building a stronger and more resilient version of yourself. You're creating a future that is filled with possibilities, a future that is truly your own.

96

Remember, your story is still being written. You are the author of your own life. Choose to rewrite your narrative. Choose to embrace a future filled with purpose, meaning, and joy. Embrace the power of your own story and step boldly into the future you've always dreamed of.

Success Stories of Transformation

The stories of those who have rewritten their narratives are inspiring testaments to the transformative power of human resilience and the potential for growth that lies within us all. These individuals, from various backgrounds and facing diverse challenges, have found ways to break free from the limitations of their past and embrace a brighter future. Their journeys offer a beacon of hope, demonstrating that it is never too late to rewrite our stories and create a life that aligns with our dreams and aspirations.

Let's explore some of these transformative tales, drawing inspiration from their journeys:

1. The Woman Who Found Her Voice:

Imagine a woman named **Payal**, living in a small village in India. For years, she had been bound by the expectations of her culture, her life meticulously planned by her family. She was expected to marry young, raise children, and dedicate herself to domestic duties. While Payal loved her family deeply, a part of her yearned for more. She felt a deep desire to express her creativity, a passion for writing that had been dormant for years. The fear of societal disapproval and the weight of tradition kept her from pursuing her dreams.

However, an unexpected turning point arrived in the form of a writing workshop organized by a local NGO. This workshop became a catalyst, igniting a spark of courage within Payal. She began to write, pouring her heart onto the pages, expressing her thoughts and dreams. Initially, it was a secret, a hidden passion she nurtured in the privacy of her room. But as her writing grew stronger, her confidence bloomed.

One day, she shared her work with a friend who encouraged her to submit it to a local magazine. To her surprise, her work was published. This act of bravery, of stepping out of her comfort zone, was the beginning of a remarkable transformation. Payal's writing found its way into national publications, her stories resonating with a wider audience. She eventually published her own collection of short stories, sharing her unique perspective on life, love, and the challenges of navigating cultural expectations.

Payal's story is a testament to the power of redefining our narratives. She defied the limitations of her past, embraced her voice, and created a future that resonated with her deepest aspirations. She became an inspiration to women in her community, proving that it is possible to rewrite our stories and create a life that is both fulfilling and true to ourselves.

2. The Entrepreneur Who Rebuilt His Life:

Rajiv, a young man from a middle-class family in Mumbai, had always dreamt of starting his own business. He was a natural innovator, with a mind brimming with ideas. He was eager to leave his mark on the world. However, life took an unexpected turn. A series of business ventures failed, leading to financial setbacks and a crushing sense of failure. The weight of these failures left him feeling lost and defeated, questioning his abilities and his path.

Instead of succumbing to despair, Rajiv decided to rewrite his narrative. He analyzed his past failures, identifying the lessons learned and the areas for improvement. He sought mentorship, surrounded himself with a supportive network of friends and family, and invested in personal development. He realized that failure was not a dead end but a steppingstone, a catalyst for growth.

With newfound clarity and determination, Rajiv embarked on a new venture. He focused on building a strong foundation, learning from past mistakes, and developing a clear vision for his business. He took calculated risks, persevering through challenges, and ultimately, his efforts bore fruit. He built a successful business that not only achieved financial success but also made a positive impact on his community.

Rajiv's story reminds us that setbacks are inevitable in life, but they need not define us. Through resilience, introspection, and a willingness to learn from our past, we can rewrite our narratives and create a future that reflects our true potential.

3. The Artist Who Embraced Healing:

Jaya, a talented painter from Bangalore, had always been deeply connected to her art. Her vibrant canvases reflected her soul, capturing the beauty and complexities of the world around her. However, a devastating personal loss plunged her into a dark abyss of grief and despair. The vibrant colors of her world seemed to fade, replaced by a somber palette of sorrow.

Jaya's art, once a source of joy and expression, became a burden, a constant reminder of her loss. She struggled to find her creative spark, her hand trembling as she held a paintbrush. It felt as if a part of her had been permanently shattered.

But Jaya, like many who have faced profound loss, found a way to heal. She embraced therapy, allowing herself to process her grief and find solace in the support of loved ones. She discovered the transformative power of art as a means of healing. Instead of shying away from her canvas, she embraced it as a safe space to explore her emotions, to channel her pain into powerful expressions.

Slowly but surely, the colors returned to her paintings, not as reminders of her loss, but as symbols of resilience, hope, and the enduring power of the human spirit. Her art became a testament to the healing journey she had undertaken, inspiring others who had experienced similar hardships.

Jaya's story underscores the profound impact of art as a means of healing and self-expression. It demonstrates that even in the face of unimaginable pain, we can find the strength to rewrite our narratives, turning our wounds into sources of inspiration and creativity.

4. The Teacher Who Found His Purpose:

Akhil, a young man from a small village in Kerala, had always dreamt of becoming a teacher. He was passionate about knowledge, eager to share his love of learning with others. However, his family, concerned about his future, discouraged him from pursuing this path. They urged him to pursue a more "practical" career, leading him to reluctantly enroll in engineering school.

For years, Akhil lived a life that felt out of sync with his true self. He excelled in his studies, but his heart wasn't in it. He found himself longing for the classroom, for the joy of guiding young minds. The weight of his family's expectations and his own sense of obligation to their dreams created an internal conflict within him.

One day, Akhil stumbled upon a program aimed at providing education to underprivileged children in rural communities. The program's mission resonated deeply with his own passion for education. He decided to take a leap of faith, leaving behind the path that society had laid out for him.

He volunteered with the program, dedicating his time and energy to educating children who had limited access to quality education. He rediscovered his passion for teaching, finding fulfillment in empowering young minds. His commitment to the program earned him recognition and respect, ultimately leading him to establish his own educational foundation.

Akhil's story exemplifies the importance of staying true to our own purpose, even when facing societal pressures or familial expectations. It reminds us that our passions are not just hobbies, but a reflection of our true selves. By embracing our passions, we can rewrite our narratives, find fulfillment in our work, and make a positive impact on the world around us.

These are just a few examples of individuals who have successfully rewritten their narratives. Their journeys demonstrate the transformative power of self-reflection, resilience, and the courage to embrace change. By learning from their experiences, we can gain valuable insights into our own stories, empowering ourselves to rewrite our narratives and create a future filled with purpose, fulfillment, and joy.

6

BUILDING RESILIENCE FOR THE FUTURE

Understanding Resilience

Resilience is the ability to bounce back from adversity, to adapt and thrive in the face of challenges. It's not about being invincible or never experiencing pain, but rather about having the mental and emotional fortitude to navigate difficulties and emerge stronger on the other side.

Imagine a mighty banyan tree, its roots deeply anchored in the earth, its branches reaching towards the sky. It has weathered countless storms, endured scorching sun and torrential rains, yet it stands tall, a testament to its resilience. Like the banyan tree, we too can develop the strength to withstand life's inevitable storms.

In the tapestry of life, we encounter various trials and tribulations. Loss, heartbreak, setbacks, disappointments, and failures – these are all part of the human experience. How we navigate these challenges determines our well-being and ultimately shapes the trajectory of our lives. Resilience is not a static trait; it's a skill we cultivate through conscious effort and practice.

Why is resilience so crucial? Because it empowers us to not only overcome adversity but also to learn and grow from it. When we face setbacks with resilience, we don't let it define us. Instead, we analyze the situation, learn from our mistakes, and use those lessons to move forward. Resilience fosters a sense of agency and control, allowing us to navigate challenges with a proactive and positive attitude.

The benefits of cultivating resilience are manifold:

Enhanced Mental Well-being: Resilience protects us from the detrimental effects of stress, anxiety, and depression. It equips us with the mental fortitude to cope with difficult situations and maintain emotional stability.

Improved Physical Health: Research suggests that resilience can have a positive impact on physical health, boosting our immune system and reducing the risk of chronic diseases.

Stronger Relationships: When we are resilient, we are better equipped to navigate the complexities of relationships. We can handle conflict constructively, offer support to others, and build deeper connections.

Increased Productivity: Resilience fuels a sense of purpose and drive, leading to improved performance in all aspects of our lives, from work to personal pursuits.

Greater Life Satisfaction: By overcoming adversity, we gain valuable insights and lessons that enrich our lives and increase our overall satisfaction.

The journey towards resilience is a personal one, a continuous process of self-discovery and growth. It's about recognizing our strengths and weaknesses, embracing our vulnerabilities, and learning to navigate life's challenges with grace and determination.

A Tapestry of Resilience

The concept of resilience is deeply embedded in Indian culture, reflected in stories, philosophies, and traditions.

The Mahabharata: The epic tale of the Mahabharata is a testament to the power of resilience. The Pandava brothers, faced with treachery and adversity, exhibit extraordinary resilience in their struggle for justice. The epic teaches us that resilience is not about giving up, but about fighting for what is right, even in the face of immense odds.

The Bhagavad Gita: This ancient Hindu scripture, a dialogue between Lord Krishna and Arjuna, emphasizes the importance of resilience and inner strength. Arjuna, overcome with fear and doubt on the battlefield, is guided by Krishna to embrace his duty and fight with courage and determination. The Bhagavad Gita encourages us to find inner strength and resilience amidst life's challenges.

The Ramayana: The story of Rama and Sita, a timeless epic of love, duty, and resilience, showcases the human spirit's ability to overcome obstacles and maintain hope, even in the face of betrayal and hardship. Rama's unwavering determination and Sita's unwavering faith in him serve as powerful examples of resilience.

These stories, woven into the fabric of Indian culture, provide timeless lessons on the importance of resilience. They remind us that adversity is not a dead end, but an opportunity for growth and transformation.

Cultivating Resilience: A Practical Approach

While resilience is often viewed as an innate quality, it's actually a skill that can be developed through conscious effort and practice.

Self-Awareness: The journey to resilience begins with self-awareness. Take the time to understand your strengths and weaknesses, identify your triggers, and recognize your patterns of thinking and behavior. This introspection is crucial for developing a proactive approach to challenges.

Mindfulness: Mindfulness, the practice of focusing on the present moment without judgment, is a powerful tool for building resilience. When you are mindful, you can observe your thoughts and feelings without getting carried away by them. This allows you to navigate challenges with greater clarity and composure.

Positive Self-Talk: Our inner voice can either empower us or hold us back. Negative self-talk can weaken our resilience, while positive self-talk strengthens it. Challenge negative thoughts and replace them with positive affirmations. Remind yourself of your strengths, past successes, and your ability to overcome challenges.

Growth Mindset: Cultivate a growth mindset, believing that your abilities can be developed through effort and dedication. This mindset fosters resilience, allowing you to embrace challenges as opportunities for learning and growth.

Seeking Support: You don't have to face challenges alone. Reach out to trusted friends, family, or a therapist for support and guidance. Surrounding yourself with a strong support system can provide the encouragement and resources you need to navigate difficulties.

Healthy Habits: Engaging in healthy habits, such as regular exercise, a balanced diet, and adequate sleep, can significantly boost your resilience. These habits improve physical and mental well-being, providing you with the energy and stamina to navigate challenges.

Gratitude: Practicing gratitude, focusing on the positive aspects of your life, can shift your perspective and enhance your resilience. When you focus on gratitude, you acknowledge the blessings in your life, even amidst difficulties, fostering a sense of hope and optimism.

Resilience in Action: Stories of Triumph

Many individuals around the world have demonstrated remarkable resilience in the face of adversity. Their stories serve as powerful inspirations, reminding us that no matter how difficult our circumstances may seem, we have the strength to overcome them.

Malala Yousafzai: This Pakistani activist, shot in the head by the Taliban for advocating for girls' education, is a symbol of resilience. She refused to be silenced and continued her fight for girls' rights around the world. Her story embodies courage, determination, and the power of hope.

Nelson Mandela: This South African anti-apartheid revolutionary spent 27 years in prison for his beliefs. He emerged with unwavering commitment to peace and reconciliation, leading South Africa towards a more just and equitable future. Mandela's story is a testament to the power of resilience and forgiveness.

J.K. Rowling: This acclaimed author faced rejection and hardship before achieving success. She persevered, using her experiences to create the beloved Harry Potter series, inspiring millions of readers around the world. Her story teaches us that resilience and determination can pave the way for remarkable achievements.

These are just a few examples of the countless individuals who have demonstrated resilience in the face of adversity. Their stories remind us that we too have the strength to overcome challenges and create fulfilling lives.

Embracing the Journey of Resilience

Building resilience is a lifelong journey, not a destination. It's about embracing the challenges that come our way, learning from them, and emerging stronger on the other side. It's about acknowledging our vulnerabilities, seeking support when needed, and cultivating a mindset of growth and optimism.

Remember, resilience is not about avoiding pain or suffering. It's about learning to navigate these experiences with grace and determination, to emerge from the storm transformed and empowered.

Let the stories of resilience inspire you, and let the lessons of Indian culture guide your journey. Embrace the challenges, cultivate inner strength, and discover the extraordinary resilience that lies within you.

Developing a Resilient Mindset

Imagine a bamboo plant, swaying gently in the breeze. It bends and flexes, adapting to the wind's force, yet remaining strong and upright. It embodies resilience, the ability to bounce back from adversity to weather storms and emerge even stronger. Just as the bamboo finds strength in its flexibility, we too can cultivate resilience in our own lives, embracing the ebb and flow of life's challenges with grace and determination.

Developing a resilient mindset isn't about becoming invincible; it's about cultivating a sense of inner strength and adaptability. It's about recognizing that life is a journey filled with ups and downs, and that our ability to navigate these challenges is what truly defines our growth. The path to resilience is paved with self-awareness, acceptance, and a willingness to learn from our experiences, both positive and negative.

Think of resilience as a muscle; it strengthens through consistent exercise. This exercise involves actively challenging our limiting beliefs, reframing our perspectives, and embracing challenges as opportunities for growth. Just as we train our bodies to endure physical exertion, we can train our minds to endure emotional and mental setbacks.

Cultivating a Resilient Mindset: Practical Strategies

Here are some practical strategies you can implement to cultivate a resilient mindset:

1. Mindfulness and Self-Awareness: At the heart of resilience lies self-awareness. Mindfulness allows us to become more attuned to our thoughts, feelings, and bodily sensations. By practicing mindfulness, we can observe our reactions to stressful situations without judgment. This awareness helps us identify patterns of thought or behavior that may be hindering our resilience. Consider incorporating mindfulness techniques like meditation, deep breathing exercises, or mindful walking into your daily routine.

2. Cognitive Reframing: Our thoughts shape our reality. Often, the way we perceive events can significantly impact our emotional response. Cognitive reframing is the art of challenging negative thoughts and reinterpreting them in a more constructive light. For example, instead of viewing a setback as a failure, see it as a learning opportunity. Instead of focusing on what you've lost, focus on what you've gained from the experience. It's about finding the silver lining in every cloud, developing a more positive and growth-oriented perspective.

3. Positive Affirmations: Positive affirmations are like mental mantras that can help reprogram our subconscious mind. They are powerful tools for building self-confidence and resilience. By regularly repeating positive statements about our strengths, abilities, and worth, we can begin to believe in ourselves more fully. Choose affirmations that resonate with you and your goals. For example, *"I am capable of overcoming any obstacle,"* or *"I am strong, resilient, and resourceful."* Repeat these affirmations daily, especially during moments of doubt or stress.

4. Building a Supportive Network: Resilience isn't a solitary endeavor; it thrives in the presence of a supportive network. Surround yourself with people who uplift you, encourage you, and offer a listening ear. This could include family, friends, mentors, or support groups. Sharing your challenges with others can help you gain new perspectives and find strength in shared experiences. Remember, you're not alone on this journey. Lean on your network for support and encouragement when facing adversity.

5. Embracing Imperfection: We all make mistakes, experience setbacks, and face challenges. The key to resilience is learning to embrace our imperfections and to view them as opportunities for growth. Don't be afraid to acknowledge your mistakes and learn from them. Focus on the lessons you can glean from each experience, rather than dwelling on the perceived failures.

6. Developing a Growth Mindset: A growth mindset is crucial for resilience. It's the belief that our abilities are not fixed but can be developed through effort, perseverance, and a willingness to learn. When we adopt a growth mindset, we view challenges as opportunities to learn and grow. We're more open to feedback, eager to embrace new experiences, and less afraid of making mistakes.

7. Setting Realistic Expectations: One of the pitfalls of resilience is setting unrealistic expectations. It's important to remember that life isn't a linear path to success. There will be setbacks, disappointments, and unforeseen challenges along the way. Setting realistic expectations can help us avoid feeling overwhelmed and discouraged when things don't go exactly as planned. Focus on progress, not perfection.

8. Practicing Self-Compassion: In the face of adversity, it's crucial to treat ourselves with kindness and understanding. Self-compassion is about acknowledging our pain and suffering without judgment or criticism. When we are hard on ourselves, we create an internal environment of self-doubt and negativity, which can hinder our resilience. Instead, practice self-kindness and remind yourself that everyone experiences setbacks; it's a part of the human experience.

9. Developing a Sense of Purpose: A sense of purpose provides direction and motivation, especially during challenging times. It's about understanding what gives your life meaning and what you want to contribute to the world. Having a sense of purpose can help you stay focused on your goals and persevere even when things get tough. Consider your values, passions, and what truly matters to you. Find ways to align your daily actions with your purpose, and you'll find a deeper sense of fulfillment and resilience.

10. Finding Meaning in Adversity: Resilience isn't just about surviving; it's about finding meaning in our challenges. When we encounter setbacks, we can choose to view them as opportunities for growth, learning, and transformation. Ask yourself, "What can I learn from this experience? How can I use this challenge to become a better version of myself?" By reframing adversity, we can find strength and purpose even in the darkest of times.

<u>The Power of Resilience in Action</u>

Let's explore some real-life examples of individuals who have demonstrated remarkable resilience in the face of adversity. These stories illustrate how the strategies discussed above can be applied in practical ways:

A. The Story of Ruhi: Ruhi was a young woman who dreamed of becoming a doctor. She faced numerous challenges, including financial difficulties, family pressure to pursue a more "traditional" career path, and the fear of failure. However, Ruhi refused to give up on her dream. She worked tirelessly, taking on multiple part-time jobs to pay for her education, and she sought out mentors who believed in her. Ruhi's resilience was fueled by her strong belief in her abilities, her unwavering determination, and her supportive network. Despite the obstacles, Ruhi persevered and ultimately achieved her goal of becoming a doctor.

B. The Story of Akash: Akash, a talented musician, experienced a devastating setback when he lost his hearing in a tragic accident. He felt lost and hopeless, questioning his identity and his future. However, Akash refused to succumb to despair. He leaned on his supportive family, sought therapy, and discovered a new passion for composing music for the visually impaired. Through his resilience and determination, Akash found new meaning in his life and used his challenges to help others.

C. The Story of Devi: Devi, a single mother, faced an overwhelming series of challenges, including financial hardship, a health crisis, and the pressures of raising her children alone. Despite these hardships, Devi maintained a positive outlook. She utilized her resourcefulness to find solutions, embraced her challenges as opportunities for growth, and cultivated a strong support network. Through her resilience, Devi found strength in her adversity and created a better life for herself and her children.

These stories demonstrate that resilience is not a trait reserved for a select few; it is a quality that can be cultivated within each of us. By applying the strategies we've discussed, we can develop our own inner strength and adaptability, allowing us to navigate life's challenges with grace, purpose, and unwavering determination. Remember, the path to resilience is not always easy, but it is a journey worth taking, for it leads to a life of strength, growth, and fulfillment.

Learning from Setbacks

Life throws curveballs. It's an inevitable part of the human experience. The trick isn't to avoid them, but to learn how to dance with them. Setbacks, failures, disappointments, they all sting, there's no denying that. But in the grand scheme of things, they can be the catalysts for our greatest growth. Think of them as steppingstones, not stumbling blocks.

Imagine a seasoned potter, their hands weathered and their eyes wise. They've seen countless pieces crack, crumble, and shatter in the kiln. But they don't throw away the broken shards in despair. Instead, they see them as an opportunity. Those fractured pieces tell a story, a story of resilience, of perseverance. The potter gathers those fragments, carefully mends them, and transforms them into something even more beautiful, a testament to the strength born from adversity.

Similarly, our setbacks, those seemingly broken pieces of our lives, hold the potential for incredible transformation. They are not failures, but rather valuable lessons waiting to be learned. The key is to embrace this perspective, to shift our mindset from seeing them as defeats to recognizing them as steppingstones on our path to growth.

How do we do this? By viewing setbacks through the lens of learning. When we encounter a setback, we must resist the urge to dwell on the pain and the what ifs. Instead, we must ask ourselves, "What can I learn from this experience? What can I take away from this situation that will make me stronger, wiser, and more capable in the future?"

Let's delve into some practical ways to cultivate this mindset of learning from setbacks:

1. Embrace the Power of Curiosity:

Curiosity is the key to unlocking the wisdom hidden within our setbacks. It's about approaching these challenges with an open mind, asking questions, and seeking understanding instead of assigning blame. Instead of focusing on why things went wrong, ask yourself, "What can I learn from this? How can I use this experience to my advantage?"

<u>Example</u>: Imagine you've been working hard towards a goal, only to be met with rejection or disappointment. Instead of letting the sting of the setback define you, turn your attention to the lessons it holds. Perhaps you realize the importance of seeking constructive feedback, or perhaps you discover a need to refine your approach. By embracing curiosity, you transform a setback into a valuable opportunity for growth.

2. Seek Out the Lessons:

Every setback, no matter how painful, offers a chance to learn and grow. It's about digging deeper, examining the situation from multiple angles, and uncovering the underlying reasons behind the setback.

<u>Example</u>: Let's say you face a professional challenge, perhaps a project that didn't meet expectations. Instead of dwelling on the failure, ask yourself, "What went wrong? What could I have done differently? What skills or knowledge do I need to develop to avoid similar setbacks in the future?"

3. Turn Setbacks into Opportunities for Innovation:

Setbacks often force us to think outside the box. They push us beyond our comfort zones and invite us to explore new solutions. Embrace this challenge as a chance to innovate, to find a different path, and to emerge stronger than before.

<u>Example</u>: Imagine you've invested time and energy into a project that fails to gain traction. Instead of viewing it as a wasted effort, see it as an opportunity to re-evaluate your strategy. Maybe you need to adapt your approach, target a different audience, or refine your messaging. By embracing innovation, you transform a setback into a springboard for success.

4. Embrace the Power of Reflection:

After a setback, take the time to reflect on the experience. Journaling can be an invaluable tool for this process. Ask yourself questions like:

What were the contributing factors to the setback?

What did I learn from this experience?

What can I do differently next time?

What are the positive aspects of this experience that I can carry forward?

Through this process of introspection, you will gain a deeper understanding of yourself and your strengths, enabling you to navigate future challenges with greater confidence and resilience.

5. Don't Be Afraid to Ask for Help:

Seeking guidance from others is a sign of strength, not weakness. When faced with a setback, don't hesitate to reach out to trusted mentors, friends, or family members for support and advice. Their perspectives can offer fresh insights and help you navigate through challenging times.

6. Practice Self-Compassion:

The most important ingredient in resilience is self-compassion. It's about treating yourself with kindness and understanding, especially during difficult times. Avoid self-criticism and harsh judgment. Instead, embrace your vulnerabilities, acknowledge your emotions, and remind yourself that you are capable of overcoming challenges.

Example: If you've made a mistake, instead of beating yourself up over it, recognize that everyone makes mistakes. Acknowledge the effort you've put in and remind yourself that you have the capacity to learn from this experience and move forward.

7. Focus on the Present:

Dwelling on the past, replaying mistakes, or worrying about the future will only hinder your progress. Instead, cultivate a sense of presence. Focus on the here and now, on the things you can control. Engage in activities that bring you joy and purpose, and find ways to practice mindfulness in your daily life.

Example: If you're feeling discouraged by a setback, take a moment to appreciate the beauty around you. Notice the feeling of the sun on your skin, the sound of birds singing, or the warmth of a cup of tea in your hand. Ground yourself in the present moment and remind yourself that you are capable of creating a better future.

8. Celebrate Your Wins, Big and Small:

Every step forward, every small victory, is worth celebrating. Recognize your progress and acknowledge your accomplishments. This will boost your confidence and reinforce your belief in your ability to overcome challenges.

<u>Example</u>: Perhaps you've taken a small step towards achieving a goal after a setback. Maybe you've learned a new skill or made a positive change in your life. Celebrate these wins, no matter how small they may seem. They are evidence of your resilience and your commitment to growth.

Remember, setbacks are not failures; they are opportunities to learn, grow, and emerge stronger than before. Embrace the journey, learn from the experiences, and never stop striving for the best version of yourself.

The Role of Support System

The strength of a tree isn't just in its roots but also in the way it stands tall against the wind, drawing nourishment from the surrounding environment. Resilience, in the human spirit, is similar. It's not just about overcoming individual challenges but also about the support system that helps us stand strong during life's storms.

Think of a tightly woven tapestry. Each thread contributes to its strength and beauty. Similarly, our personal resilience is woven from the threads of our relationships – our family, friends, mentors, and even the broader community we belong to. These connections are not merely sources of comfort but powerful forces that help us weather life's hardships.

Imagine a young woman named **Tara**, burdened by the weight of societal expectations. She felt trapped in a life meticulously planned by her family, a path she didn't truly desire. However, her resilience found its strength in her close-knit group of friends. They provided her with a safe space to explore her aspirations, challenge her limiting beliefs, and discover her own unique path. This group of friends, her chosen family, became the bedrock of her resilience, encouraging her to break free from the shackles of societal norms and embrace her true self.

Our support systems, whether they be family, friends, or chosen communities, offer a multitude of benefits that bolster our resilience:

Emotional Support: They offer a safe haven where we can express our vulnerabilities and process our emotions. It's within these spaces that we can feel truly seen, heard, and understood, easing the burden of carrying our struggles alone.

Practical Assistance: They provide tangible help when we need it most. Whether it's lending a shoulder to cry on during a heartbreak or offering a helping hand during a difficult time, their practical support can ease the weight of our challenges.

Perspective and Guidance: They offer a different lens through which to view our problems, helping us see beyond the immediate crisis and gain clarity. Their insights and guidance can illuminate paths we might not have seen on our own.

Sense of Belonging: They create a sense of community and belonging, reminding us that we are not alone in our journey. Knowing that we are part of a network of individuals who care for us strengthens our resolve and helps us overcome difficult times.

However, cultivating supportive relationships isn't always easy. We may face challenges like:

Distance and Limited Contact: Life's circumstances may lead us to be geographically distanced from loved ones. Maintaining strong connections over time can be challenging, requiring conscious effort and regular communication.

Differing Values and Beliefs: We may find ourselves at odds with family members or friends due to varying values or beliefs. Navigating these differences requires open and respectful communication and a willingness to understand and accept each other's perspectives.

Building New Connections: Sometimes, we find ourselves in new environments where building meaningful connections from scratch can be daunting. However, actively engaging in our communities, seeking out shared interests, and being open to new relationships can create a sense of belonging.

Here are some practical tips to cultivate supportive relationships that bolster resilience:

Nurture Existing Connections: Make time for the people who matter most. Regularly check in, engage in meaningful conversations, and show your appreciation for their presence in your life.

Extend Kindness and Support: Just as we need support, others do too. Be a source of strength for those around you, offering a listening ear, a helping hand, or words of encouragement.

Engage in Community Activities: Join groups, clubs, or organizations that resonate with your interests. These shared activities provide a platform for connecting with others who share similar passions.

Practice Active Listening: When connecting with others, truly listen with an open mind and heart. Empathetically understand their perspectives and offer your support in a way that feels genuine and helpful.

Seek Professional Help When Needed: Sometimes, we may need professional support to process past trauma or navigate difficult emotional challenges. Therapists and counselors can provide a safe and confidential space to explore our feelings and develop strategies for growth.

Building resilience is a continuous process, like a journey that unfolds over time. It's a path that requires ongoing effort, self-awareness, and the strength of supportive relationships. As we navigate life's challenges, remember that we are not alone. Our support systems, like the roots of a strong tree, provide the foundation for weathering storms and blossoming into the best versions of ourselves.

Resilience in Action

Resilience, the ability to bounce back from adversity, is an essential life skill, especially when navigating the complexities of the past. It's the inner strength that allows us to weather storms, learn from our falls, and rise again, stronger and wiser. It's not about being impervious to pain or challenges; it's about how we respond to them. Resilience is a choice, a conscious decision to find meaning and purpose even in the face of hardship. It's a journey of self-discovery, a testament to the human spirit's capacity for growth and renewal.

The journey of resilience is often paved with stories – stories of individuals who have stared into the abyss of adversity and emerged triumphant. These stories are beacons of hope, reminders that even in the darkest of times, there's a light within us that can guide us towards a brighter future. Let's delve into a few such narratives, each a unique testament to the human spirit's extraordinary resilience.

From Ashes to Embers: The Story of a Businesswoman

In the heart of Mumbai, amidst the bustling chaos of India's financial capital, stood a woman named **Tina**. She had built a successful business from scratch, her entrepreneurial spirit fueled by a burning ambition and a relentless work ethic. But life, in its unpredictable nature, had a different plan. A sudden economic downturn swept across the country, leaving Tina's business on the brink of collapse. The once-thriving enterprise crumbled, leaving her with nothing but a mountain of debt and the crushing weight of failure.

The world around Tina seemed to shrink, the vibrant city turning into a desolate landscape of despair. The dreams she had held so dearly, the vision she had nurtured, lay in ruins. This wasn't just a business failure; it was a personal blow, a challenge to her very identity. The whispers of doubt echoed in her mind, "What's the point?" they asked. "You've failed. You've lost everything."

But Tina, despite the crushing weight of her losses, refused to succumb to despair. She remembered a quote she had once read: "The difference between ordinary and extraordinary is that little extra." That extra, she realized, was resilience. She refused to let the past define her. Instead, she chose to learn from her mistakes, to see the setback as an opportunity for growth.

With renewed determination, Tina sought support, she sought guidance from mentors, and she delved into self-reflection. She identified her strengths and weaknesses, pinpointing the areas where she could improve. She re-evaluated her business model, adapting it to the changing market conditions.

It wasn't an easy path. There were days when the darkness threatened to consume her, days when the whispers of doubt grew louder, but Tina persevered. She drew strength from the support of her loved ones, from the inner fire that refused to be extinguished.

Slowly, painstakingly, she rebuilt her business. It wasn't the same enterprise, but it was hers, born out of the ashes of her past failures. Her journey taught her the importance of adaptability, of learning from mistakes, and of harnessing the power of resilience. She had risen from the ashes, her spirit tempered by the fires of adversity.

The Dance of Tradition and Ambition: A Story of Cultural Reconciliation

In a small village nestled in the foothills of the Himalayas, lived a young woman named **Kiran**. She had always felt a pull towards the vibrant world beyond the village, a longing to break free from the confines of tradition. Anjali dreamed of becoming a doctor, of using her knowledge to heal and to make a difference in the lives of others. This dream, however, clashed with the deeply rooted cultural norms of her village.

In her community, girls were expected to marry young, to prioritize family and domestic life. The pursuit of higher education, especially in a profession outside the traditional roles, was seen as a deviation from the path laid out by generations. Kiran's ambition faced resistance, a chorus of whispers and disapproving glances, a pressure to conform to the expectations that had shaped the lives of countless women before her.

The conflict between her dream and her community's expectations created a chasm within Kiran, a tension that threatened to tear her apart. She was torn between her desire to honor her family and the unwavering belief in her own potential.

Kiran's resilience lay in her ability to navigate this complex terrain. She chose not to abandon her dream but to find a way to reconcile it with her cultural identity. She engaged in open dialogues with her family, explaining her aspirations and the passion that fueled them. She sought out mentors who had successfully balanced traditional values with personal goals. She used her community's strengths, its emphasis on values like respect and perseverance, as fuel for her own journey.

It wasn't easy. There were moments of doubt, moments of frustration, but Kiran persevered. She used her cultural background as a source of strength, her roots providing the grounding she needed to push forward. She demonstrated her commitment through her hard work, her dedication to her studies, and her unwavering belief in her dream.

Ultimately, Kiran's resilience allowed her to bridge the gap between tradition and ambition. She received her education, fulfilling her dream, while simultaneously upholding the values she held dear. She became a symbol of hope in her community, an inspiration to young women who dared to dream beyond the confines of tradition. She proved that resilience isn't about discarding one's roots; it's about finding ways to grow while honoring them.

From Loss to Liberation: A Story of Healing and Acceptance

Deep in the heart of Kerala, in a village known for its lush greenery and the rhythm of life that flowed with the ebb and flow of the backwaters, lived a young man named **Ravi**. Ravi was a talented musician, his soul filled with the music of his heritage, his fingers dancing across the strings of his veena, weaving melodies that captured the essence of his land. But fate, in a cruel twist, snatched away his beloved wife, leaving Ravi shattered and lost.

The world around him blurred, the vibrant colors of life fading into shades of gray. The music that had been his solace now echoed with the pain of his loss, a constant reminder of what he had lost. Ravi retreated into a shell of grief, his spirit broken, his will to live waning.

Ravi's journey towards resilience was paved with grief, with moments of despair so profound they threatened to consume him. But he had a deep-rooted faith, a belief in the power of acceptance. He knew that dwelling in his pain would only prolong the suffering.

He sought solace in his music, using it to express his grief, to process the raw emotions that overwhelmed him. He found solace in his community, in the love and support of his family and friends. He embraced the healing power of nature, spending hours by the serene backwaters, allowing the gentle rhythm of the water to soothe his troubled soul.

The road to healing was long and arduous. There were days when the pain felt unbearable, days when the memories of his loss threatened to engulf him. But Ravi never gave up. He held onto the hope that there was light at the end of the tunnel, that he could find joy and meaning in life again.

With time and with the support of his loved ones, Ravi began to emerge from the shadows of grief. He discovered that while he couldn't erase the pain of his loss, he could find a way to live with it. He chose to honor his wife's memory by living a life filled with purpose and meaning. He found joy in sharing his music, in connecting with others through the universal language of melody.

Ravi's journey taught him the power of acceptance, the importance of finding meaning in life's challenges, and the enduring power of hope. He emerged from the darkness of grief, not unscathed, but transformed, his spirit tempered by the fires of loss, his resilience forged in the crucible of pain.

Beyond the Stories: The Essence of Resilience

These stories, though unique in their details, share a common thread. They are testaments to the indomitable human spirit, to our capacity to overcome adversity, to rise from the ashes of hardship. These narratives offer valuable lessons for us all, reminding us that resilience is not an innate quality but a skill that can be developed, nurtured, and strengthened.

Resilience is about embracing the present moment, acknowledging our pain, and choosing to move forward. It's about finding meaning and purpose even in the midst of challenges, recognizing that setbacks are often steppingstones to growth. It's about building a support system, surrounding ourselves with people who can lift us up when we fall, who remind us of our inner strength.

The journey of resilience is not always smooth, but it is always worth the effort. By learning from the stories of others, by understanding the essence of resilience, we can equip ourselves with the tools to face life's challenges with courage, grace, and unwavering determination. For in the end, it is our resilience that allows us to navigate the complexities of the past, to embrace the present, and to create a future filled with hope and possibility.

7

CULTURAL NORMS AND PERSONAL GROWTH

The Balance of Tradition and Change

The tapestry of Indian culture is rich with traditions that have been passed down through generations, offering wisdom and guidance on living a fulfilling life. These customs, often deeply rooted in family values and religious beliefs, provide a sense of belonging and continuity. However, navigating the complexities of modern life while honoring these traditions can be a delicate balancing act.

As individuals seek personal growth, they may find themselves at a crossroads where their desires for self-discovery clash with the expectations of their culture. It's in these moments that the concept of "being Indian" can feel like a tightrope walk, where tradition and change exist in a constant tug-of-war.

Imagine a young woman, **Asha**, growing up in a traditional Indian family. She is expected to pursue a stable career in medicine, a path her parents have carefully laid out for her. However, Asha's heart yearns for a career in creative writing, a field seen as unconventional and unpredictable within her community. She feels a conflict between honoring her family's wishes and pursuing her own passion.

Asha's story is not unique. Many individuals from diverse cultural backgrounds grapple with similar challenges. They might feel pressured to follow a specific career path, adhere to strict social norms, or prioritize arranged marriages over finding love on their own terms. This tug-of-war between personal desires and cultural expectations can lead to feelings of guilt, confusion, and even rebellion.

However, the key lies in recognizing that personal growth and cultural respect are not mutually exclusive. It's possible to embrace the values and traditions that have shaped us while also carving out space for our own aspirations and choices. This journey requires a mindful approach, open communication, and a willingness to bridge the gap between tradition and change.

<u>Here are some practical ways to navigate this delicate balance:</u>

1. Understanding Cultural Values:

<u>Reflect on Your Roots:</u> Take the time to understand the reasons behind your cultural norms. What values are they based on? Why are they important to your family and community? Understanding the underlying principles can help you appreciate the significance of these traditions even if you choose to diverge from them.

<u>Engage in Dialogue:</u> Speak openly with your family, elders, and other respected members of your community. Ask questions about their perspectives and values. Engage in respectful dialogue to gain a deeper understanding of their views and learn from their experiences.

2. Defining Your Personal Values:

<u>Introspection and Self-Discovery:</u> Take a journey inward to identify your core values and aspirations. What matters most to you? What do you truly desire in life? Be honest with yourself about your dreams and goals, regardless of what others expect.

<u>Balancing Tradition and Change:</u> Recognize that change is inevitable. Cultures evolve over time, and individuals must adapt to changing circumstances. Seek a balance between upholding the values that matter most to you and embracing opportunities for personal growth.

3. Communicating Your Choices:

<u>Respectful Transparency:</u> Communicate your choices and aspirations clearly and respectfully. Share your motivations and the importance of these choices to you. Be prepared to explain how your choices align with the values you share with your family and community.

<u>Finding Common Ground:</u> Seek common ground with your loved ones. Focus on the values you share, such as respect, hard work, and family unity. Show them that your personal growth does not diminish your respect for

tradition.

4. Embracing Cultural Strengths:

Leveraging Heritage: Identify the strengths and qualities instilled in you through your culture. Use these qualities to fuel your personal growth. For example, if your culture emphasizes hard work and resilience, leverage these qualities to overcome challenges and achieve your goals.

Sharing Your Journey: Share your journey of personal growth with your family and community. Explain how your experiences have shaped your values and how you continue to honor your cultural heritage in new ways.

5. Building a Personal Culture:

Creating Your Own Path: Remember that your journey is unique. You can create your own culture, one that blends the traditions you hold dear with your personal aspirations and values. This allows you to honor your roots while embracing your individuality.

Living Authentically: Be true to yourself. Don't feel pressured to conform to unrealistic expectations or to sacrifice your dreams for the sake of tradition. Live a life that aligns with your authentic self, while respecting the values that have shaped you.

Remember, navigating the balance between tradition and change is an ongoing process. It requires empathy, understanding, and a willingness to communicate openly. The journey might not always be smooth, but it's through this process of navigating cultural norms and personal growth that we discover who we truly are and create a life that is both fulfilling and meaningful.

Stories of Cultural Navigation:

Here are some real-life examples of individuals who have successfully navigated the balance between tradition and change:

Aisha, a talented chef, grew up in a family that emphasized arranged marriages. While respecting her family's values, she also felt a strong desire to find a partner who shared her passion for cooking and travel. Aisha bravely expressed her feelings to her family, emphasizing her desire to build a life with someone who understood her dreams. With open communication and a willingness to compromise, Aisha was able to find a loving partner who supported her culinary aspirations. Her story demonstrates the power of honest dialogue and mutual respect in navigating cultural norms.

Raman, an aspiring artist, faced pressure from his family to pursue a more "stable" career path. However, he refused to let go of his passion for art. Raman found creative ways to express his artistic talents while respecting his family's concerns. He started a side business creating custom artwork, gradually gaining recognition and financial stability. His journey highlights the importance of finding ways to blend personal passions with family expectations, creating a path that honors both tradition and individual aspirations.

These stories, along with Asha's journey, showcase the diverse ways individuals can navigate the complexities of culture and personal growth. The key lies in recognizing that tradition and change are not incompatible. By understanding your cultural roots, defining your personal values, communicating effectively, and embracing cultural strengths, you can create a life that honors your heritage while allowing you to pursue your unique path.

<u>Challenging Cultural Expectations</u>

The tapestry of our lives is woven with threads of tradition and personal aspirations. In the vibrant hues of Indian culture, we find ourselves navigating the delicate dance between honoring cherished customs and pursuing our individual paths. While tradition serves as a bedrock of identity and community, it can sometimes impose limitations, dictating roles and expectations that may not align with our personal growth. This chapter explores the art of challenging cultural expectations, finding a harmonious balance between tradition and personal fulfillment.

Imagine a young woman named **Nisha**, raised in a family deeply rooted in traditional values. Her dreams lie beyond the confines of societal expectations, yearning to pursue a career in science, a field often considered unconventional for women in her community. Nisha faces a dilemma: how to honor her family's traditions while chasing her aspirations. She grapples with the weight of societal norms, the whispers of doubt, and the fear of disappointing those she loves.

Nisha's story reflects a common struggle, a tug-of-war between cultural expectations and personal desires. While honoring tradition is essential for a sense of belonging and continuity, clinging rigidly to outdated norms can stifle our growth and limit our potential. Finding a middle ground, a path of mindful evolution, becomes paramount.

Understanding the Roots of Cultural Expectations

Cultural norms, deeply ingrained in the fabric of our societies, serve as guiding principles for behavior, beliefs, and values. They shape our understanding of the world, influencing our choices, aspirations, and interactions. While these norms often foster a sense of community and identity, they can also act as invisible barriers, imposing limits on individual expression and aspirations.

The roots of cultural expectations lie in a complex interplay of historical, societal, and religious factors. In India, for instance, the tradition of arranged marriages has long been a cornerstone of family and community life, ensuring continuity and stability. Similarly, certain professions, like medicine and law, have traditionally been considered more suitable for men, while women were often expected to prioritize domestic duties. These expectations, while deeply ingrained in the cultural fabric, may not always resonate with individual aspirations and may create conflict between personal desires and societal pressures.

Navigating the Labyrinth of Expectations

The journey of challenging cultural expectations can feel like navigating a labyrinth, with a multitude of paths leading to different outcomes. This journey demands courage, self-awareness, and a deep understanding of both our personal values and the cultural context we inhabit.

1. Self-Reflection and Awareness:

The first step in this journey involves introspection, taking a deep dive into our own values, aspirations, and fears. What are our personal goals? What traditions hold significance for us, and which ones feel limiting? By examining our beliefs and desires, we can identify the specific areas where cultural expectations clash with our personal aspirations.

2. Open Dialogue and Communication:

Open and respectful communication plays a vital role in bridging the gap between personal growth and cultural expectations. Sharing our aspirations with our families, friends, and communities can foster understanding and create space for meaningful dialogues. It's important to approach these conversations with empathy, recognizing that generational differences and differing perspectives may exist.

3. Finding Common Ground:

While challenging outdated norms, it's crucial to remember the underlying values and principles that underpin cultural expectations. Often, a shared value system forms the foundation of traditional practices. For instance, the value of family in Indian culture can be expressed in numerous ways, extending beyond the traditional structure of arranged marriages. By finding common ground, we can honor the essence of cultural values while pursuing our own paths.

4. Embracing Gradual Change:

Change, especially in the realm of cultural norms, rarely happens overnight. Gradual evolution, fostering understanding and dialogue, often proves more effective than abrupt revolutions. As we strive to challenge limiting expectations, it's essential to recognize the importance of patience, respect, and a willingness to compromise.

5. Finding Your Voice:

Standing up for your beliefs and pursuing your aspirations requires finding your voice. This can be a daunting task, but it's essential to learn to articulate your desires, address concerns, and advocate for your right to personal growth. By speaking your truth, we empower ourselves to navigate the labyrinth of cultural expectations and create a path that aligns with our values.

Examples of Cultural Navigation

The stories of individuals who have successfully balanced cultural expectations with personal growth provide inspiration and guidance.

Padma, the Aspiring Scientist:

Padma's journey is a testament to the power of open communication and compromise. Through candid conversations with her family, she explained her passion for science and her desire to pursue a career in this field. While initially met with skepticism, her unwavering determination, coupled with her commitment to honoring family traditions, eventually earned her support. Padma found ways to blend her aspirations with cultural expectations, volunteering at local clinics and sharing her knowledge with younger girls in her community, demonstrating that a scientific career could complement her family's values.

Rajan, the Entrepreneur:

Rajan, hailing from a family of doctors, felt an undeniable pull towards entrepreneurship. His family, deeply rooted in the medical profession, initially viewed his aspirations with apprehension. Rajan, however, approached this challenge with empathy and understanding. He recognized the importance of respecting his family's traditions while pursuing his own path. He engaged in thoughtful conversations, highlighting the benefits of entrepreneurship and the potential for contributing to the family's legacy in new and innovative ways. Rajan's commitment to his family's values, coupled with his entrepreneurial spirit, paved the way for his success.

Creating a Personal Culture

As we journey through life, we inevitably shape our own unique blend of values, beliefs, and practices. This personal culture becomes a reflection of our experiences, aspirations, and the lessons we learn along the way.

1. Defining Your Values:

At the heart of our personal culture lie our core values—the principles that guide our actions, beliefs, and decisions. These values might be rooted in cultural traditions, personal experiences, or spiritual beliefs. By defining our values, we create a foundation upon which we can build a life that aligns with our deepest aspirations.

2. Embracing Your Uniqueness:

Each of us possesses a unique blend of talents, passions, and perspectives. This uniqueness, shaped by our personal experiences and cultural influences, is a valuable asset. Embracing our individuality allows us to create a personal culture that reflects our true selves.

3. Building a Positive Narrative:

Our personal culture is built upon the stories we tell ourselves and the narratives we create. By fostering a positive narrative, focusing on our strengths, and learning from our setbacks, we can cultivate a sense of self-worth and confidence.

4. Honoring Traditions with a Modern Twist:

Our personal culture can integrate cherished traditions with a modern twist, finding innovative ways to express our cultural heritage while aligning with our individual aspirations.

5. Continuous Evolution:

Our personal culture is not static; it evolves with our experiences, growth, and the lessons we learn along the way. Remaining open to change, embracing new perspectives, and adapting to evolving circumstances are essential for creating a personal culture that continues to reflect our values and aspirations.

<u>Conclusion</u>

The journey of challenging cultural expectations requires courage, self-awareness, and a willingness to embrace change. By fostering open communication, finding common ground, and embracing gradual evolution, we can navigate the delicate dance between tradition and personal growth. Ultimately, our goal is to create a personal culture that honors our heritage while empowering us to live a fulfilling and authentic life. Just as the vibrant colors of a sunset blend seamlessly, so too can we harmonize the richness of our cultural heritage with the pursuit of our individual dreams.

Embracing Cultural Strengths

The Indian cultural fabric is rich with tradition, wisdom, and a profound understanding of the human experience. Within this tapestry lies a wealth of knowledge that can serve as a compass for personal growth. By recognizing and embracing these cultural strengths, we can navigate the complexities of life with a greater sense of purpose and direction.

One such strength is the concept of **"Vasudhaiva Kutumbakam,"** which translates to "the whole world is one family." This powerful principle encourages us to view ourselves as part of a larger interconnected web, fostering a sense of unity and shared responsibility. In our quest for personal growth, embracing this concept can help us cultivate empathy, compassion, and a deeper understanding of the human condition.

Another invaluable cultural strength is the emphasis on **"Satya,"** truthfulness. The pursuit of truth is a central pillar of Indian philosophy, encouraging us to strive for honesty and integrity in our thoughts, words, and actions. By embodying this principle, we cultivate a sense of inner peace and clarity, paving the way for genuine connections and ethical decision-making.

Furthermore, the Indian concept of **"Dharma,"** or righteous duty, provides a framework for living a meaningful life. Dharma emphasizes the importance of fulfilling our obligations to ourselves, our families, our communities, and the world at large. Recognizing our individual Dharma can guide us towards a path of service and purpose, aligning our actions with our values and contributing to the well-being of others.

The practice of **"Yoga,"** both physical and philosophical, is another significant cultural strength. Yoga, with its focus on physical postures, breathing techniques, and meditation, provides a holistic approach to well-being. It cultivates mindfulness, flexibility, and inner peace, allowing us to connect with our inner selves and achieve a sense of balance and harmony.

In addition, Indian culture emphasizes the value of **"Karma,"** the principle of cause and effect. By understanding the concept of Karma, we recognize the consequences of our actions and strive to create positive ripple effects in the world. This understanding empowers us to take responsibility for our choices, cultivate a sense of purpose, and contribute to the betterment of society.

These cultural strengths, when integrated into our personal growth journey, can provide valuable insights and guidance. The concept of "Vasudhaiva Kutumbakam" fosters empathy and understanding, while "Satya" guides us toward truthfulness and integrity. "Dharma" encourages us to live a life of purpose and service, and "Yoga" cultivates mindfulness and inner peace. "Karma" empowers us to take responsibility for our actions and create a positive impact on the world.

By embracing these cultural strengths, we can tap into a reservoir of wisdom and insight that transcends generations. We can create a more mindful, compassionate, and purposeful approach to personal growth, aligning our actions with our values and contributing to a more harmonious and just world.

As we navigate the complexities of modern life, it is essential to find balance between honoring traditions and embracing change. We can draw inspiration from the wisdom of the past while simultaneously embracing the dynamism and opportunities of the present. We can leverage the strengths of our cultural heritage to create a vibrant and meaningful life, one that honors both tradition and progress.

In embracing the rich tapestry of Indian culture, we can find a path that leads to personal growth, inner peace, and a deeper connection to ourselves and the world around us. This journey of self-discovery, enriched by the wisdom and values of our heritage, can empower us to live a life that is both fulfilling and impactful.

Stories of Cultural Navigation

The tapestry of Indian culture is woven with threads of tradition, customs, and expectations that have been passed down for generations. While these cultural norms offer a sense of belonging and identity, they can sometimes create a complex dance between personal growth and societal expectations. Navigating this intricate balance is a journey that many individuals in India, and across the globe, find themselves on.

Let's explore this journey through the stories of individuals who have found their own unique ways to honor their cultural roots while embracing personal growth.

The Story of Meera:

Meera, a bright young woman from a traditional family in Mumbai, always dreamt of becoming a doctor. Her parents, however, had different plans for her. They envisioned her following in her grandmother's footsteps and becoming a renowned classical dancer. While Meera held immense respect for her family's traditions, her heart belonged to medicine. The clash between her aspirations and her family's expectations created a deep internal conflict.

Meera's journey was marked by quiet resistance. She diligently practiced dance, honoring her parents' wishes while secretly attending medical school classes at night. The weight of her double life was heavy, but her passion for medicine fueled her determination. Eventually, her talent and hard work caught the attention of a renowned physician who saw her potential.

With his support, Meera found the courage to confront her parents. She explained her passion for medicine, highlighting the importance of pursuing her dreams while still honoring their traditions. The conversation was difficult, but Meera's genuine passion and commitment ultimately swayed her parents. They understood her yearning for a life that aligned with her own values, and they offered their support.

Meera's story exemplifies the power of finding a balance between tradition and personal growth. It reminds us that honoring cultural expectations doesn't have to mean sacrificing our dreams. Instead, it often involves finding creative ways to integrate our aspirations within the framework of our cultural heritage.

The Journey of Ajit:

Ajit, a young man from Delhi, grew up with the expectation of pursuing a career in his family's successful business. From a tender age, he was groomed to take over the reins of the enterprise. However, Ajit harbored a different ambition – he yearned to become a writer. This divergence from the traditional path fueled a silent struggle within him.

Ajit's journey started with a hesitant exploration of his passion. He began writing in secret, late at night, fearing judgment and disapproval. He found solace in expressing himself through words, a form of escape from the confines of his expected future. His writing served as a bridge between his cultural obligations and his personal aspirations.

As Ajit honed his craft, his work began to gain recognition. He started receiving invitations to literary events, and his writing became a source of pride for his family, albeit one they initially didn't understand. The turning point came when Ajit's work was published in a national newspaper. His family, seeing his talent and passion, finally embraced his dream. They realized that Ajit's success as a writer was not a betrayal of their legacy, but a unique expression of their family's values.

Ajit's story illustrates the transformative power of embracing one's true calling, even if it deviates from traditional expectations. It showcases how personal growth can be nurtured within the context of a rich cultural heritage, leading to a fulfilling life that honors both tradition and individual aspirations.

The Story of Vani:

Vani, a young woman from a small village in Kerala, grew up surrounded by strong familial traditions. Her family had always been involved in agriculture, and she was expected to follow in their footsteps. However, Vani's heart belonged to the world of technology. She dreamt of becoming a software engineer, a path that seemed distant and inconceivable within the confines of her village.

Vani's journey was filled with determination and resilience. She started by learning basic computer skills at a local community center, fueled by a burning desire to bridge the gap between her aspirations and her cultural context. She then sought out opportunities for higher education in a nearby city, where she excelled in her studies.

While Vani faced initial resistance from her family, who feared she was abandoning their traditions, her dedication and achievements gradually convinced them. They saw in her a future that combined the values of their heritage with the opportunities offered by the modern world.

Vani's story highlights the importance of perseverance in pursuing personal growth. It reminds us that even in societies deeply rooted in tradition, there is space for innovation and personal fulfillment. It also underscores the significance of education and knowledge as tools for navigating cultural expectations and shaping one's own future.

A Shared Thread:

The stories of Meera, Ajit, and Vani, despite their diverse backgrounds, share a common thread: the unwavering pursuit of personal growth while respecting and honoring their cultural roots. They show us that navigating cultural norms and personal aspirations is not a binary choice; it's a delicate dance of finding a balance that respects the past while embracing the present.

Beyond Individual Stories:

These stories go beyond individual experiences. They represent a broader societal shift in India and across the globe. As societies become increasingly globalized, individuals are grappling with the complexities of balancing cultural expectations with personal growth. This is not a conflict to be avoided but a dynamic process to be navigated with intention, understanding, and respect.

The Essence of Cultural Navigation:

At its core, cultural navigation is about finding a sense of belonging within a changing world. It's about understanding and appreciating the richness of our cultural heritage while also embracing the opportunities for personal growth that lie beyond its boundaries.

It's about finding a way to live a life that aligns with our values, honoring our traditions while creating a future that is uniquely our own.

Key Takeaways:

Respect and Appreciation: Cultural navigation begins with a deep respect and appreciation for our cultural heritage. It's about understanding the traditions, values, and beliefs that shape our identity.

Open Dialogue: Open and honest communication is crucial for navigating cultural expectations. Engaging in dialogues with family members, mentors, and communities can help bridge the gap between tradition and personal growth.

Creative Solutions: Finding creative solutions is often essential when it comes to balancing cultural expectations with personal aspirations. Exploring innovative ways to integrate our dreams within the framework of our heritage can lead to a fulfilling path.

Resilience and Perseverance: Navigating cultural norms often requires resilience and perseverance. We may face challenges, resistance, or even setbacks along the way, but it's crucial to stay committed to our journey.

Empowerment and Agency: Cultural navigation is about empowering ourselves to shape our own destinies. It's about recognizing that we have the agency to make choices that align with our values and aspirations.

<u>A Legacy of Growth:</u>

In conclusion, cultural navigation is a journey of self-discovery, a process of finding our place in the world while honoring our cultural roots. It's not about choosing between tradition and change but rather finding a balance that respects the past while embracing the present. The stories of Meera, Ajit, and Vani provide a roadmap for this journey, showcasing the resilience, creativity, and determination needed to navigate the complexities of cultural expectations and personal growth. As we learn from their experiences, we can embrace the power of cultural navigation to create a fulfilling and meaningful life that honors our heritage and empowers us to reach our full potential.

Creating a Personal Culture

Imagine a tapestry woven with vibrant threads of tradition, customs, and beliefs. This is the rich fabric of our culture, a heritage we inherit and carry within us. It shapes our values, our aspirations, and even the way we perceive the world. Yet, as we navigate the complexities of life, we may find ourselves at a crossroads, where the pull of tradition clashes with the yearning for personal growth.

This is where the concept of building a "personal culture" comes into play. It's about recognizing the influence of our cultural norms while creating a unique set of values and beliefs that guide our choices and define our own path.

Think of it as a personal compass. Our cultural heritage provides the framework, the map, and the stories that shaped us. But as we embark on our own journeys, we have the power to choose the direction, the destinations, and the adventures we pursue.

This process isn't about abandoning our cultural roots; it's about embracing them while acknowledging our individuality. It's about honoring the traditions we hold dear while carving out space for our own aspirations and dreams.

Finding Harmony Between Tradition and Change

Imagine a young woman named **Veena**, raised in a family deeply rooted in Indian tradition. Her parents, both doctors, encouraged her to pursue a career in medicine, following a familiar and respected path. However, Veena harbors a passion for art, a yearning to express herself through colors and brushstrokes.

Veena's journey is a testament to the delicate balance between tradition and change. On one hand, she deeply respects her family's values and their unwavering commitment to serving others. On the other hand, she recognizes the importance of nurturing her own passions and embracing the unique talents that make her who she is.

Priya's story exemplifies the common challenges we face when navigating our cultural heritage and personal growth. We may feel pulled in multiple directions, caught between the expectations of our families, the traditions of our community, and the desires of our own hearts.

Challenging Limiting Norms

While our cultural heritage provides a foundation for our lives, it's essential to acknowledge that some societal norms can be limiting. These norms may dictate specific roles, expectations, or beliefs that restrict our choices and hinder our growth.

For instance, a young man named **Pavan**, raised in a rural village in India, is expected to follow in his father's footsteps and become a farmer. However, Pavan dreams of pursuing a career in technology, driven by a fascination with computers and innovation.

Pavan's situation highlights the importance of questioning limiting norms. He may face resistance from his family and community, but his unwavering belief in his own potential and his willingness to challenge societal expectations pave the way for his own growth.

Embracing Cultural Strengths

While some cultural norms may limit our choices, it's important to recognize the strengths and resources that our heritage offers. These cultural strengths can act as powerful tools for personal growth and development.

For example, a young woman named **Ganga**, raised in a family that values strong work ethic, discipline, and perseverance, finds these traits immensely valuable in her pursuit of her career. The values instilled in her through her cultural upbringing fuel her determination and drive, allowing her to overcome challenges and achieve success.

Ganga's story demonstrates how cultural values can provide a foundation for personal growth. By recognizing and leveraging these strengths, we can tap into a wealth of wisdom, resilience, and support that our heritage provides.

Creating a Personal Culture

The journey of creating a personal culture is a continuous process of introspection, exploration, and self-discovery. It involves identifying our core values, defining our goals, and forging a path that aligns with both our cultural heritage and our personal aspirations.

<u>Here are some practical steps to embark on this transformative journey:</u>

1. Reflect on Your Values: Take time to reflect on the values that are most important to you. These may be values instilled by your family, your community, or your personal experiences.

2. Define Your Goals: Identify your short-term and long-term goals. What do you want to achieve in life? What kind of person do you aspire to be?

3. Embrace Your Individuality: Recognize and celebrate the unique qualities that make you who you are. Your individuality is a gift, a valuable asset on your journey of personal growth.

4. Seek Out Mentors and Support: Surround yourself with people who inspire you, challenge you, and support your journey. Mentors can guide you through challenges, provide advice, and offer encouragement.

5. Be Open to Change: Change is a constant in life. Be open to learning, evolving, and adapting as you navigate your personal journey. Embrace new experiences, expand your horizons, and never stop growing.

Cultural Navigation Stories

Throughout history, countless individuals have navigated the complexities of tradition and personal growth. Their stories offer insights, inspiration, and a sense of shared experience.

One such story is that of **Mahatma Gandhi,** who, while deeply rooted in Indian culture, challenged societal norms and fought for independence through nonviolent resistance. His journey embodies the courage to challenge limiting beliefs and to strive for a better world.

Another example is that of **Malala Yousafzai,** a young Pakistani activist who defied cultural norms and fought for the right of girls to receive an education. Her unwavering commitment to education and her willingness to challenge societal expectations are a beacon of hope for those seeking to create change.

These stories, and countless others, remind us that the journey of personal growth often involves navigating the complex landscape of our cultural heritage. It's a journey of finding harmony between the traditions we hold dear and the aspirations we have for ourselves.

A Living Legacy

Building a personal culture is not just about defining our own path; it's about leaving a legacy, a mark on the world that reflects our values and our journey. It's about sharing our experiences, inspiring others, and contributing to a more inclusive and enriching society.

As we embark on this journey, let us remember the words of the wise, "The best way to find yourself is to lose yourself in the service of others." By embracing our cultural heritage, challenging limiting norms, and fostering personal growth, we become beacons of inspiration for generations to come.

Let us strive to create a world where tradition and change dance together in harmony, where our personal cultures become a vibrant tapestry woven with threads of individuality, resilience, and purpose.

8

THE ROLE OF GRATTITUDE
IN MOVING FORWARD

The Science of Gratitude

Gratitude, a simple yet powerful emotion, has been recognized for centuries as a key to happiness and well-being. But in recent years, scientific research has begun to unravel the profound impact of gratitude on our minds and bodies, providing solid evidence for its transformative power.

Imagine a world where you are consistently overwhelmed by negativity, where every setback is a crushing blow and every inconvenience feels like a personal attack. It's easy to get stuck in this downward spiral, constantly dwelling on what's missing or what's gone wrong. But what if there was a way to shift your perspective, to train your mind to focus on the good, the beautiful, and the positive? This is where the science of gratitude comes into play.

Gratitude is not just about being thankful for material possessions or grand gestures; it's about cultivating an appreciation for the small, everyday things that bring joy and meaning to life. It's about recognizing the goodness that surrounds us, even in the midst of challenges.

Studies have shown that gratitude can have a profound impact on our mental and emotional well-being. It can:

Reduce stress and anxiety: When we focus on what we are grateful for, we shift our attention away from negative thoughts and worries, creating a sense of calm and peace.

Boost happiness and optimism: By appreciating the good in our lives, we cultivate a more positive outlook, enhancing our overall sense of well-being.

Improve physical health: Research suggests that gratitude can strengthen the immune system, reduce blood pressure, and improve sleep quality.

Strengthen relationships: Expressing gratitude to others strengthens bonds, fostering feelings of connection and belonging.

Increase resilience: By acknowledging our blessings, we develop a greater capacity to cope with adversity, making us more resilient in the face of challenges.

But how does gratitude actually work? Scientists believe that gratitude activates a specific set of neural pathways in the brain, triggering the release of dopamine, serotonin, and other neurotransmitters associated with pleasure, contentment, and well-being. This chemical cascade helps us feel happier, more optimistic, and more connected to others.

The benefits of gratitude extend beyond the individual. When we express gratitude to others, it can have a ripple effect, spreading positivity and creating a more harmonious environment. A simple "thank you" can make someone's day, while a heartfelt expression of appreciation can strengthen relationships and build trust.

In the context of Indian culture, gratitude is deeply ingrained in the fabric of life. From ancient texts like the Bhagavad Gita to modern practices like the daily "Aarti," gratitude is seen as a virtue that fosters harmony, connection, and inner peace. This emphasis on gratitude is not simply a cultural norm; it's a reflection of the profound understanding of its transformative power.

But practicing gratitude doesn't require grand gestures or elaborate rituals. It can be as simple as taking a moment to appreciate the beauty of a sunset, the warmth of a loved one's embrace, or the simple joy of a cup of tea.

<u>Here are some practical ways to incorporate gratitude into your daily life:</u>

Keep a gratitude journal: Take a few minutes each day to write down three things you are grateful for. This simple practice can help you focus on the positive aspects of your life and shift your perspective.

Express gratitude to others: Make a conscious effort to express your appreciation to people who have made a positive impact on your life. Whether it's a thank-you note, a phone call, or a simple gesture, your gratitude will be noticed and appreciated.

Practice mindful meditation: Meditation can help you cultivate an attitude of gratitude by focusing your attention on the present moment and appreciating the small things.

Engage in acts of kindness: Helping others is a wonderful way to cultivate gratitude, as it reminds you of the abundance in your own life.

Find beauty in the ordinary: Pay attention to the beauty in everyday moments, whether it's the sunlight filtering through the trees, the sound of birds singing, or the simple act of breathing.

Express gratitude for challenges: It may seem counterintuitive, but even challenging experiences can teach us valuable lessons and contribute to our growth. By expressing gratitude for the lessons learned, we can transform negative experiences into positive ones.

The path to living fully in the present, free from the shackles of the past, requires more than just recognizing the weight of our yesterdays. It requires actively cultivating a grateful heart, one that finds joy in the present, embraces the lessons of the past, and looks forward to the possibilities of the future.

By incorporating these simple practices into your daily life, you can unlock the transformative power of gratitude and begin to experience a deeper sense of peace, contentment, and fulfillment. Remember, gratitude is not simply an emotion; it's a conscious choice, a way of life that can lead you towards a more fulfilling and joyful existence.

<u>Daily Gratitude Practices</u>

Imagine a life where you wake up each morning with a sense of deep contentment, a feeling of appreciation for the simple blessings that surround you. This isn't a fantasy; it's the power of gratitude, a potent force that can transform your outlook and enrich every aspect of your existence. In the tapestry of life, gratitude acts as a vibrant thread, weaving together the threads of joy, resilience, and fulfillment.

The practice of gratitude is not just a fleeting sentiment; it's a deliberate choice, a conscious act of acknowledging the good in our lives. It's about recognizing the gifts, both big and small, that we often overlook in our daily rush. It's about appreciating the beauty of a sunrise, the warmth of a hug, the taste of a delicious meal, the comfort of a cozy bed.

Think of gratitude as a mental lens that focuses our attention on the positive aspects of our lives. It's a mental shift from dwelling on what's missing to embracing what we have. This shift in perspective can significantly impact our emotional well-being, allowing us to navigate life's challenges with greater resilience and optimism.

So, how do we cultivate this powerful state of gratitude? The key lies in making it a daily practice, weaving it seamlessly into the fabric of our routines. It's not about grand gestures; it's about the little things that make a big difference. It's about creating a daily ritual of appreciation, a moment to pause and reflect on the blessings that surround us.

<u>Here are a few simple yet effective practices you can incorporate into your daily life to nurture a heart full of gratitude:</u>

1. The Gratitude Journal: This is a classic practice that involves keeping a notebook or using a digital app where you jot down three things you are grateful for each day. It can be anything from the warmth of the sun on your skin to a kind gesture from a stranger to the laughter of your loved ones. It doesn't have to be profound; what matters is that you consciously recognize and appreciate the good things in your life.

2. The Gratitude Walk: Take a moment each day to step outside, away from the hustle and bustle of everyday life. As you walk, engage all your senses— notice the colors of the leaves, the sounds of birds chirping, the scent of blooming flowers, the feel of the breeze on your skin. Allow these sensory experiences to fill you with appreciation for the beauty of the natural world.

3. The Gratitude Meditation: Incorporate a few minutes of gratitude meditation into your daily routine. You can do this by simply sitting or lying down in a comfortable position, closing your eyes, and focusing on your breath. As you breathe, mentally list the things you are grateful for. Let the feeling of appreciation wash over you, filling you with warmth and contentment.

4. The Gratitude Dinner: Make it a practice to express gratitude during your meals. Before you begin eating, take a moment to acknowledge the food on your plate, the people you are sharing it with, and the farmers and workers who made it possible. This simple ritual fosters appreciation for the abundance in your life.

5. The Gratitude Phone Calls: Instead of just sending a text or email, take the time to call someone you appreciate and express your gratitude. It could be a friend, a family member, a colleague, or even a stranger who has touched your life in a positive way. Let them know how much their presence or actions mean to you.

6. The Gratitude Acts of Kindness: Gratitude is not just about receiving; it's also about giving. Find ways to express your gratitude through acts of kindness. It could be volunteering your time, offering a helping hand to someone in need, or simply brightening someone's day with a smile.

7. The Gratitude Letter: Write a letter of gratitude to someone who has had a significant impact on your life. This doesn't have to be a lengthy letter; even a few heartfelt words can express your appreciation. You can choose to share the letter or keep it for yourself.

8. The Gratitude Visualization: Take a few minutes each day to visualize your life filled with abundance and happiness. Imagine yourself surrounded by the people and things you are grateful for. This visualization practice can help cultivate a more positive and grateful mindset.

9. The Gratitude Playlist: Create a playlist of music that evokes feelings of gratitude and happiness. Listen to these songs when you need a boost of positivity or when you want to reflect on the blessings in your life.

10. The Gratitude Affirmations: Incorporate gratitude affirmations into your daily routine. These are positive statements that you repeat to yourself to reinforce a grateful mindset. For example, you could say, "I am grateful for the love in my life," or "I am thankful for my good health."

As you integrate these practices into your daily life, you'll begin to notice a gradual shift in your perspective. You'll find yourself focusing more on the good, less on the bad. You'll experience a greater sense of contentment, even amidst life's challenges.

Gratitude is a powerful force that can unlock a life filled with joy, fulfillment, and resilience. It's not about ignoring the negative; it's about choosing to focus on the positive, to appreciate the beauty that surrounds us, and to recognize the blessings that we often take for granted.

Remember, cultivating gratitude is an ongoing journey, a constant practice of appreciation. It's about embracing the little things, the everyday moments that make life extraordinary. It's about finding the good, even in the midst of hardship, and recognizing the gifts that life presents us with each and every day.

Gratitude and Positive Thinking

Imagine a field of sunflowers, each one turning its face towards the sun, absorbing its warmth and light. This is a simple image, yet it carries a profound metaphor for the power of gratitude. Just as sunflowers draw strength from the sun, we can draw strength and joy from the countless blessings in our lives.

Gratitude, like a gentle breeze, can shift the way we perceive the world. It can transform our outlook from one of scarcity to one of abundance. By cultivating a grateful heart, we cultivate a positive mindset, allowing us to see opportunities where we once saw only limitations.

Think of a time when you were feeling down, perhaps burdened by the weight of past regrets. In those moments, it's easy to fall into the trap of focusing on the negative, magnifying our challenges and overlooking the good things around us. But what if we shifted our attention? What if, instead of dwelling on what we lacked, we focused on what we had?

This is the essence of gratitude: recognizing and appreciating the good things in our lives, no matter how small they may seem. It's about finding the silver lining in the clouds, the spark of hope in the darkness. It's about choosing to see the world through a lens of appreciation rather than one of negativity.

There's a beautiful Indian proverb that captures the power of gratitude: "If you have food in your stomach, a roof over your head, and a place to sleep, you are richer than 75% of the world." This proverb reminds us that even in the face of challenges, we have much to be grateful for.

How does gratitude foster a positive mindset? It's a simple yet powerful mechanism. When we practice gratitude, our brains release feel-good hormones like dopamine and serotonin, promoting a sense of well-being and happiness. This positive emotional state, in turn, allows us to approach life with a more optimistic lens, seeing possibilities instead of limitations.

Consider the example of a young woman named **Lata**, who was struggling to find her place in a society that expected her to conform to traditional expectations. She felt trapped by the weight of her family's expectations, feeling inadequate and lost. But then she discovered the transformative power of gratitude.

Lata began focusing on the small blessings in her life: her loving family, her close-knit community, the beauty of nature, and the gift of good health. She started journaling about her gratitude, noting each day the things she was thankful for. As she practiced gratitude, a profound shift took place within her.

She began to see her challenges not as obstacles but as opportunities for growth. She realized that her family's expectations, though sometimes overwhelming, stemmed from their love and concern. She discovered that she could honor her heritage while pursuing her own dreams, finding a balance between tradition and personal fulfillment.

Lata's journey underscores the transformative power of gratitude. It's not about ignoring the challenges or denying our pain. Instead, it's about expanding our awareness to see the beauty and goodness that surrounds us, even in the midst of difficulties.

The practice of gratitude can be simple yet profound. It doesn't require grand gestures or elaborate rituals. Start by taking a few minutes each day to reflect on the things you are grateful for, however small they may seem. You can keep a gratitude journal, write a thank-you note to someone who has touched your life, or simply take a moment to appreciate the warmth of the sun on your skin.

By cultivating a habit of gratitude, we cultivate a positive mindset that attracts abundance, joy, and fulfillment into our lives. We shift our focus from what we lack to what we have, from scarcity to abundance, from negativity to positivity.

Remember the sunflowers, turning their faces towards the sun. Let us, too, turn our hearts towards gratitude, allowing its warmth to fill our lives with light and joy.

153

Transformative Stories of gratitude

The power of gratitude extends far beyond a mere feeling of thankfulness. It's a transformative force that can reshape our lives, ushering in positivity, resilience, and a renewed sense of purpose. Gratitude acts as a beacon, illuminating the beauty in our everyday experiences and guiding us towards a more fulfilling life. To truly grasp its potency, we must delve into the stories of individuals who have witnessed its power firsthand.

Imagine a young woman named **Mayuri**, burdened by the weight of her past. She had spent years dwelling on the painful memory of a failed relationship, allowing it to dictate her decisions and overshadow her present happiness. Fearful of venturing into a new love, she shielded herself from potential connections, convinced that any attempt at intimacy would only lead to heartbreak. Her past was a prison, and she felt trapped within its confines.

One day, during a particularly gloomy period, Mayuri stumbled upon a quote about the transformative power of gratitude. Intrigued, she decided to give it a try. Each evening, she would jot down three things she was grateful for, no matter how small. Initially, it felt forced, an artificial exercise. But as she continued, a subtle shift began to occur.

The simple act of focusing on the positive aspects of her life – the warmth of the sun on her skin, the comforting aroma of her mother's cooking, the laughter shared with her friends – created a ripple effect. Slowly, the darkness that had enveloped her began to recede. The gratitude journal became a lifeline, reminding her of the good in her life, even during challenging times. As she embraced gratitude, Mayuri discovered a profound sense of peace and contentment. Her heart, once burdened by the past, started to open up to new possibilities. The fear of heartbreak gradually dissipated, replaced by a newfound optimism. She realized that her past, while painful, did not define her. It was simply a chapter in her story, a lesson learned, a catalyst for growth.

Empowered by gratitude, Mayuri decided to take a leap of faith and open herself up to new connections. She signed up for a dance class, a pursuit she had always been passionate about but had shied away from due to fear. In the studio, surrounded by others who shared her love for movement and expression, Mayuri felt a sense of belonging she had long missed. She found joy in the present moment, reveling in the beauty of the dance, the camaraderie of her fellow dancers, and the exhilaration of pushing her limits.

As Mayuri deepened her practice of gratitude, her life began to blossom in ways she never thought possible. She discovered new passions, forged meaningful connections, and embraced opportunities she had previously deemed unattainable. The shadow of her past had lifted, replaced by a radiant glow of hope and gratitude.

Another compelling story of transformation through gratitude unfolds in the life of **Rajat**, a young man grappling with a challenging career trajectory. He had always harbored a deep desire to pursue his passion for photography, but societal pressures and the need for a stable income had led him down a path he felt unfulfilled by. He worked long hours in a corporate job that drained his energy and left him feeling uninspired. The weight of his unfulfilled dreams created a heavy burden, fueling a sense of dissatisfaction and resentment towards his situation.

One day, Rajat stumbled upon an article about the transformative power of gratitude, specifically in overcoming professional challenges. Intrigued, he began incorporating gratitude practices into his daily routine. Every morning, before heading to work, he would take a few minutes to reflect on the things he was grateful for: his health, his loving family, his safe home, and the small joys that punctuated his day, such as a delicious cup of chai or a conversation with a friend.

Initially, Rajat found it difficult to focus on gratitude when his mind was consumed by anxieties about his career path. However, he persisted, determined to cultivate a more positive perspective. As he diligently practiced gratitude, he began to notice a shift in his outlook. The overwhelming sense of dissatisfaction began to fade, replaced by a newfound appreciation for the good things in his life. He started noticing the beauty in the mundane – the warmth of the sun on his skin as he walked to work, the laughter of children playing in the park, the comforting routine of his daily rituals.

The realization that he had much to be thankful for empowered Rohan to take control of his situation. He began dedicating his evenings to his passion, attending photography workshops, practicing his skills, and connecting with other photographers. The fire that had been smoldering within him was rekindled, ignited by the spark of gratitude.

As Rajat embraced his passion with renewed vigor, his career began to take an unexpected turn. A friend, impressed by his work, introduced him to a local magazine editor, who was seeking a photographer for an upcoming project. This opportunity opened doors to a new world of creative possibilities, and Rajat was able to transition into a career that aligned with his true passions. His journey, fueled by gratitude, served as a powerful reminder that even in the face of adversity, a shift in perspective can lead to transformative growth.

These stories are but two examples of the countless lives touched by the power of gratitude. It has the remarkable ability to shift our focus from what we lack to what we have, transforming our perception of ourselves and the world around us. Gratitude acts as a catalyst for personal growth, empowering us to let go of past grievances, embrace the present, and step confidently towards a future filled with possibilities.

The practice of gratitude is not about denying the challenges we face or overlooking the pain of our past. It's about acknowledging both the light and the shadows in our lives, recognizing that even in the darkest of times, there are always reasons to be grateful.

Gratitude can be a powerful antidote to negativity, a source of strength in the face of adversity, and a beacon of hope that guides us towards a more fulfilling and meaningful life. It's a simple yet profound practice that can transform our lives one moment at a time.

<u>Building a Gratitude Habit</u>

Gratitude is not just a fleeting emotion; it's a transformative power that can shift our perspectives, ignite our joy, and empower us to move forward with renewed hope. It's a powerful antidote to the negativity that can often accompany dwelling in the past. When we practice gratitude, we make a conscious decision to focus on the positive aspects of our lives, even amidst challenges. This simple act of acknowledging the good in our lives can have a profound impact on our emotional well-being, fostering resilience and optimism.

Imagine a garden. Over time, weeds can take over, choking out the vibrant flowers and healthy plants. Similarly, our minds can become overgrown with negative thoughts and past regrets, overshadowing the beauty and potential of our present lives. Gratitude acts as a gardener, carefully tending to the soil of our minds, pulling out the weeds of negativity and nurturing the seeds of joy, hope, and appreciation.

Cultivating a habit of gratitude is a journey, not a destination. It's about consistently making the effort to notice and appreciate the good things in our lives, no matter how small they may seem. Just as a gardener patiently tends to their plot, we must be patient and persistent in our practice, allowing the seeds of gratitude to take root and flourish.

<u>Steps to Nurture a Gratitude Habit:</u>

1. Start Small: Begin by focusing on a few things you're grateful for each day. It could be anything, from a warm cup of tea in the morning to a kind gesture from a stranger. Write them down in a journal, share them with loved ones, or simply take a moment to reflect on them.

2. Embrace a Gratitude Ritual: Incorporate gratitude into your daily routine. It could be as simple as starting your day with a few moments of quiet reflection, expressing gratitude for your health, loved ones, or the simple act of waking up. You might also end your day with a gratitude journal entry, reflecting on the positive experiences you've had throughout the day.

3. Find Meaning in Every Moment: Look for the good in everyday occurrences, even the mundane ones. Instead of focusing on traffic jams, be grateful for the opportunity to listen to your favorite music or catch up on podcasts. Be present in your daily activities, noticing the little things that bring you joy.

4. Express Your Gratitude: Let others know how much you appreciate them. Sending a handwritten note, making a phone call, or simply expressing your gratitude verbally can deepen connections and spread positive energy.

5. Visualize Your Gratitude: Close your eyes and imagine yourself surrounded by all the things you're grateful for. Visualize the people you love, the experiences that have enriched your life, and the blessings you hold dear. This visualization can help strengthen your feelings of gratitude and bring a sense of peace.

6. Embrace Gratitude in Challenging Times: Gratitude can be a powerful tool even when facing difficult circumstances. Remember that even during tough times, there are still things to be grateful for – your health, your loved ones, or the lessons you're learning.

The Power of a Grateful Heart:

Increased Happiness and Well-being: Studies have shown that practicing gratitude can significantly boost our overall happiness and well-being. When we focus on the positive aspects of our lives, we naturally feel more optimistic and content.

Enhanced Resilience: Gratitude helps us cope with stress and adversity by shifting our focus from what we lack to what we have. It strengthens our inner resources, enabling us to navigate challenges with more grace and fortitude.

Improved Relationships: Expressing gratitude to others strengthens our connections and deepens our bonds. It shows people that we appreciate their presence in our lives, fostering a sense of warmth and appreciation.

Increased Productivity: Gratitude can enhance our motivation and focus. When we feel grateful for what we have, we're more likely to be energized and engaged in our work and personal endeavors.

A Shift in Perspective: Gratitude fosters a more positive outlook on life. It helps us see the good in every situation, even when it's hard to find. This shift in perspective can transform our entire world view, leading to a more fulfilling and joyful experience.

The Story of Sudha and the Tiny Seed:

Sudha, a young woman living in a bustling city, was struggling. The weight of her past failures, career setbacks, and strained relationships cast a shadow over her life. She felt trapped by the constant replays of disappointment, unable to see a path forward.

One day, while walking through a crowded marketplace, Sudha stumbled upon a tiny, fragile seed tucked into a small clay pot. It was a simple, unassuming seed, but it held a powerful message. The vendor, a wise old man, said, "This seed represents gratitude. Plant it in your heart, and it will blossom into a beautiful life filled with joy and abundance."

Intrigued, Sudha took the seed home and decided to give it a chance. She planted it in a tiny pot on her windowsill and diligently cared for it. Every morning, she'd spend a few moments reflecting on things she was grateful for, whispering her gratitude to the tiny sprout.

At first, Sudha found it difficult to find things to be grateful for. She was so overwhelmed by her own anxieties and disappointments. But as she persisted in her practice, she began to notice small things that brought her joy – the warmth of the morning sun, the gentle breeze rustling through the leaves, a kind word from a stranger.

Slowly, with each passing day, the tiny seed started to sprout. It grew steadily, pushing through the soil with an unwavering determination. Sudha watched with wonder as the fragile sprout transformed into a vibrant plant, its leaves reaching towards the sun with a newfound strength.

As the plant grew taller, so did Sudha's sense of gratitude. She began to see her own life through a more positive lens, recognizing the beauty and blessings that had always been present. She realized that her past failures were not a definition of her worth, but rather stepping stones on her path to growth.

With renewed hope and a grateful heart, Sudha embraced the present moment. She started making positive changes in her life, focusing on her strengths and pursuing her passions. The tiny seed had blossomed into a powerful symbol of transformation, reminding her that gratitude is not just an emotion, but a way of life.

<u>Cultivating Gratitude, Cultivating a Brighter Future:</u>

The journey of gratitude is a lifelong adventure, a constant exploration of the good that surrounds us. It's about finding joy in the everyday, embracing our blessings, and cultivating a more positive outlook on life.

As we nurture a habit of gratitude, we empower ourselves to move forward with newfound strength, resilience, and a deep appreciation for the beauty of life, regardless of the challenges we may face. Like Maya's tiny seed, our gratitude can blossom into a vibrant, joyful life, filled with hope, purpose, and a profound sense of contentment.

9

EMBRACING NEW BEGININGS

Fear of the Unknown

The fear of the unknown is a primal instinct, a whisper in the back of our minds that warns us against venturing into the unfamiliar. It's a natural response to the discomfort of stepping outside our comfort zones, a yearning for the familiar and the predictable. This fear can manifest in various forms, from the apprehension of starting a new job to the trepidation of embarking on a new relationship or even the daunting prospect of a move to a new city.

In the context of embracing new beginnings, this fear can be particularly potent. It often arises from the uncertainty of what lies ahead, the anxiety of facing the unknown, and the nagging doubt that we might not be able to handle the challenges that await. However, it is crucial to recognize that the fear of the unknown is not inherently bad. It is a vital part of our survival instincts, a signal that tells us to be cautious and to assess the situation before we plunge into unfamiliar territory.

The key lies in understanding and managing this fear rather than letting it paralyze us. It is through embracing the uncomfortable, stepping outside our comfort zones, and challenging the limitations we impose on ourselves that we truly grow.

Think of the fear of the unknown as a bridge, a necessary stepping stone between the familiar and the new. It's a bridge that requires us to confront our anxieties, to acknowledge the discomfort, and to find the courage to cross over. But on the other side, we find something extraordinary – a world of possibility, a chance to reinvent ourselves, to explore new horizons, and to discover the hidden potential within us.

In the tapestry of Indian culture, the concept of **"shunya"** – emptiness or void – offers a compelling metaphor for understanding and embracing the fear of the unknown. Shunya, in its essence, represents a state of potentiality, a blank canvas that holds the promise of boundless possibilities. Just as a painter approaches a blank canvas with a sense of anticipation and excitement, we can embrace the fear of the unknown with a similar perspective. It is not a void to be feared, but a space to be filled with our courage, our aspirations, and our willingness to embrace the unknown.

<u>Here's how to navigate the fear of the unknown and turn it into a catalyst for growth:</u>

1. Acknowledge and Embrace the Fear:

The first step towards overcoming any fear is to acknowledge its presence. Don't try to suppress or ignore it. Instead, allow yourself to feel the fear, to recognize its intensity, and to understand where it stems from. This process of acknowledgment is essential for gaining a sense of control over your emotions. Remember, fear is a natural response, and by embracing it, you are not surrendering to it; you are acknowledging its existence and giving yourself the space to confront it.

2. Understand the Root of Your Fear:

Once you've acknowledged the fear, take some time to reflect on its root cause. Is it a fear of failure, a fear of judgment, a fear of the unknown, or a fear of change? The more you understand the specific source of your fear, the better equipped you will be to address it.

For instance, if your fear stems from past failures, try to identify the lessons learned from those experiences and how you can apply them to the new beginning. If your fear is fueled by a lack of confidence, consider ways to build your self-esteem and develop a stronger sense of self-worth. By pinpointing the root of your fear, you can address it directly, creating a more solid foundation for your journey ahead.

3. Challenge Your Limiting Beliefs:

The fear of the unknown often feeds on limiting beliefs, negative thoughts, and self-doubt. These limiting beliefs can manifest in self-defeating statements like, "I'm not good enough," "I can't handle this," or "I'm going to fail." It's crucial to identify these beliefs and challenge them.

Ask yourself: What evidence supports these beliefs? Are they based on facts or on assumptions? Replace negative thoughts with more positive and empowering ones. Replace "I can't" with "I can" and "I'm not good enough" with "I am capable." By challenging these limiting beliefs, you create a mental space for growth and opportunity.

4. Embrace the Power of Curiosity:

Instead of focusing on the potential dangers of the unknown, shift your perspective towards curiosity. Instead of asking, "What if I fail?" ask "What if I succeed?" Instead of focusing on the potential challenges, focus on the potential opportunities. Embrace a sense of exploration, a willingness to discover the wonders that lie ahead, and a curiosity to learn and grow along the way.

Think of the unknown as a treasure chest filled with experiences, lessons, and discoveries waiting to be unearthed. Approach it with a sense of wonder and a spirit of adventure, and you'll find that the journey itself becomes a source of joy and fulfillment.

5. Seek Inspiration and Support:

Surround yourself with people who believe in you and who encourage you to embrace new beginnings. Seek inspiration from others who have overcome their fears and achieved their dreams. Read stories of resilience, of people who have ventured into the unknown and emerged stronger and more fulfilled. Their journeys can serve as powerful reminders that you too can overcome your fears and create a life that is both meaningful and fulfilling.

6. Start Small and Celebrate Successes:

When facing the unknown, it's important to start small. Break down your goals into manageable steps, celebrate every milestone achieved, and gradually build your confidence and resilience. These small victories, however insignificant they may seem, are crucial stepping stones on your path to embracing new beginnings.

7. Practice Gratitude and Mindfulness:

Gratitude is a powerful antidote to fear. When you focus on what you are grateful for, it shifts your perspective, reminding you of the good in your life and fostering a sense of peace and optimism. Mindfulness, on the other hand, helps you stay present in the moment, allowing you to recognize and manage your emotions without getting carried away by fear. Both gratitude and mindfulness are essential tools for navigating the challenges of embracing new beginnings.

8. Embrace the Imperfection:

There is no such thing as a perfect new beginning. Life is a journey of constant change, and there will be moments of uncertainty, doubt, and setbacks. Embrace the imperfections, acknowledge that you are not always going to get things right, and learn from your mistakes. It is through these challenges and failures that you grow and evolve.

9. Focus on the Journey, Not Just the Destination:

It's easy to get caught up in the end goal, the idealized picture of success. But remember that the journey itself is just as important. Enjoy the process of growth, the challenges you overcome, the lessons you learn, and the new experiences you acquire along the way. The destination is simply a marker on the road, a signpost that points towards a future filled with potential.

Embrace the fear of the unknown. See it as a challenge to be overcome, a bridge to be crossed, and a blank canvas to be filled with possibilities. Let it guide you, inspire you, and empower you to create a life that is both meaningful and fulfilling.

Taking the First Step

Taking the first step is often the most daunting aspect of embarking on a new journey. The fear of the unknown, the weight of past failures, and the lingering comfort of familiar routines can all conspire to keep us anchored in the past. But, just like the first step on a long and winding road, the initial move towards a new beginning is the catalyst for transformative change. It's the moment you decide to break free from the shackles of the past and embrace the promise of a brighter future.

Imagine a young woman named **Dipika**, steeped in the traditions of her family, who had always dreamt of becoming a doctor. However, societal expectations and the pressure to conform to traditional roles had led her down a different path. She had married young, fulfilling the wishes of her parents, and was now expected to dedicate her life to her family and home. While Dipika loved her family dearly, a part of her yearned for the life she had envisioned. The weight of unfulfilled dreams and the fear of defying societal norms kept her tethered to her current reality.

One day, while browsing through a local bookstore, she stumbled upon a book about personal growth and self-discovery. The book's message resonated deeply with her, igniting a spark of hope. It spoke of the power of dreams and the importance of pursuing one's passion, regardless of societal pressures. That book became her catalyst for change.

Inspired by the book's wisdom, Dipika began taking small but significant steps towards her dream. She started by enrolling in a part-time medical assistant program, using her free time after fulfilling her domestic responsibilities. Each night, while everyone else slept, she would study diligently, fueled by a newfound determination. Her family, though initially apprehensive, eventually understood and supported her aspirations, their initial anxieties giving way to admiration for her courage.

Dipika's journey was not without challenges. There were moments of self-doubt, when the exhaustion of balancing family responsibilities with studies threatened to overwhelm her. But she persevered, drawing strength from the dreams she had dared to resurrect. The fear of failure transformed into a potent motivator, driving her to excel in her studies.

Over time, Dipika's commitment and hard work paid off. She graduated with honors, securing a position as a medical assistant. The joy of fulfilling her long-held dream brought tears of happiness to her eyes. The journey had been arduous, but the reward was immeasurable. Dipika's story underscores the transformative power of taking that initial step, however small, towards a new beginning. It is a testament to the fact that even amidst the constraints of tradition and societal expectations, one can reclaim their dreams and carve a path towards a fulfilling life.

So how do we take that first step? How do we move beyond the fear and embrace the possibility of a fresh start? It begins with a shift in mindset, a conscious decision to break free from the limitations of the past and embrace the unknown.

<u>Here are some strategies to help you take the first step towards a new beginning:</u>

1. Identify Your Limiting Beliefs: Often, the biggest obstacle to change is not external pressures, but our own internal limitations. These are the beliefs, often ingrained from past experiences or societal conditioning, that tell us we can't achieve our dreams, or that we are not worthy of happiness.

<u>Journaling:</u> Take some time to journal about your past experiences and identify the beliefs that might be holding you back. Ask yourself questions like: "What do I believe about myself?" "What are my limiting beliefs about change?" By bringing these limiting beliefs to the surface, you can begin to challenge and dismantle them.

<u>Challenge Your Negative Self-Talk:</u> Pay attention to the internal dialogue you have with yourself. Are you constantly criticizing yourself, focusing on past failures, or dwelling on negative thoughts? Challenge these negative voices with positive affirmations. Replace "I can't" with "I can," and "I'm not good enough" with "I am capable and worthy."

<u>Seek Support:</u> Talking to a trusted friend, family member, therapist, or

counselor can provide valuable insights and help you gain perspective on your limiting beliefs. They can offer a fresh perspective and challenge your negative thoughts.

2. Embrace the Power of Small Steps: Overcoming the past and embracing a new beginning doesn't happen overnight. It's a gradual process, a journey of baby steps that lead to significant change.

Break Down Your Goals: Instead of focusing on the overwhelming task of achieving your goal in its entirety, break it down into smaller, more manageable steps. For example, if you want to start a business, break it down into tasks like researching your target market, creating a business plan, and setting up your online presence.

Focus on Daily Progress: Instead of focusing on grand achievements, celebrate the small wins along the way. Did you wake up early and exercise? Did you complete a task on your to-do list? These seemingly insignificant actions contribute to the bigger picture, and acknowledging your daily progress keeps you motivated.

Don't Be Afraid to Experiment: Embrace a spirit of experimentation and explore different approaches to achieving your goals. There is no one-size-fits-all approach to change. Be open to trying new things, learning from your experiences, and adapting your strategy as needed.

3. Cultivate a Growth Mindset: A growth mindset, as opposed to a fixed mindset, is the belief that our abilities and intelligence are not fixed but can be developed through hard work, dedication, and a willingness to learn from failures.

Embrace Challenges: Instead of viewing challenges as setbacks, embrace them as opportunities for growth and learning. Challenges are unavoidable in life, and they often lead to breakthroughs and personal development.

Learn from Mistakes: We all make mistakes, but a growth mindset views these as valuable learning experiences. Instead of dwelling on past failures, use them as opportunities to reflect, learn, and grow.

Seek Feedback: Be open to constructive feedback from others. Feedback can help you identify areas for improvement and refine your approach to reaching your goals.

4. Build a Supportive Network: Surrounding yourself with a supportive network of friends, family, mentors, or peers can make a significant difference in your journey towards a new beginning.

<u>Seek Out Mentors:</u> Mentors can provide guidance, encouragement, and insights based on their own experiences.

<u>Join a Support Group:</u> Support groups can provide a sense of community and understanding, especially if you're going through a challenging transition.

<u>Connect with Like-Minded Individuals:</u> Connecting with people who share your aspirations or interests can provide motivation, inspiration, and a sense of belonging.

Embracing a new beginning is a courageous act, a declaration that you are ready to move beyond the limitations of the past and create a future that aligns with your dreams and aspirations. It's a journey that demands courage, perseverance, and a willingness to step outside of your comfort zone. But the rewards are immeasurable: a life filled with purpose, fulfillment, and the joy of living in the present moment.

The Growth Mindset

The past, like a weathered tapestry woven with threads of joy, sorrow, triumph, and defeat, holds a powerful sway over our present lives. We often find ourselves revisiting these threads, dwelling on the triumphs that bring a bittersweet nostalgia or the defeats that leave us with lingering regret. While these memories shape our identity and inform our decisions, clinging to them can become a formidable obstacle to growth. It's like trying to move forward while carrying a heavy, unwieldy baggage – the weight of the past can hinder our ability to embrace the present and step confidently towards a fulfilling future.

Imagine a young woman named **Purvi**, raised in a traditional Indian household. From a tender age, she witnessed her family's struggles, the sacrifices made to provide for her education and future. She excelled in her studies, eventually securing a scholarship to study abroad. This opportunity, a dream she had nurtured since childhood, presented a significant departure from the life she knew. Yet, as she prepared for her departure, a sense of anxiety washed over her. The weight of her family's expectations, the fear of disappointing her parents, and the nagging fear of failing to live up to their sacrifices, held her back. She found herself caught in a web of conflicting emotions – gratitude for the opportunities she had been given, yet fear of the uncertainty ahead.

This internal conflict is not uncommon. Our past experiences, the expectations we carry from our families, our culture, and even our own past achievements, can become an invisible weight that we carry with us, shaping our beliefs and influencing our actions. It's a natural human tendency to be influenced by our past, to seek solace in familiar patterns, and to avoid the unknown. But if we're not careful, this attachment to the past can become a prison, limiting our growth and stifling our potential.

For Purvi, the fear of the unknown and the weight of expectations threatened to derail her dream. She started questioning her choices, wondering if she was making the right decision. The familiar comfort of her family, her culture, and her routine, seemed more appealing than the daunting prospect of starting anew in a foreign land. This internal struggle exemplifies the power of our past narratives, how they can color our present and cast a shadow on our future.

However, recognizing these limiting patterns is the first step towards breaking free. Just as Purvi began to question the source of her anxiety, we, too, can start to examine the narratives we tell ourselves, the beliefs that hold us back. We can begin to challenge the assumptions that we've held onto, the fears that have been passed down through generations, and the doubts that have been fueled by past experiences.

Instead of allowing the past to dictate our present and future, we can choose to adopt a growth mindset. A growth mindset embraces challenges as opportunities for learning and sees setbacks as stepping stones to greater success. It recognizes that our abilities are not fixed, but rather, capable of development through effort, persistence, and a willingness to learn from our experiences. It's like shifting from a fixed lens that only sees the limitations of the past to a broader, more dynamic perspective that embraces the possibilities of the present and the future.

For Purvi, adopting a growth mindset meant confronting her fears and acknowledging her strengths. She recognized that her education, her determination, and her unwavering support system were valuable assets, far outweighing the fears she held. She started viewing her journey abroad as a chance to grow, learn, and expand her horizons. She embraced the challenges as opportunities to learn, to adapt, and to discover new parts of herself. She began to see the unknown as a blank canvas, a canvas on which she could paint her own future, unburdened by the past.

Adopting a growth mindset doesn't mean forgetting our past, nor does it mean discarding the valuable lessons it offers. It means choosing to learn from our experiences, embracing the power of our past narratives to inform, but not define, our present and future. It means accepting the fact that we can change, grow, and evolve, and that we have the power to shape our own destiny.

The journey from a fixed mindset to a growth mindset can be challenging, but it's a journey worth embarking upon. It's about letting go of the baggage of the past, embracing the transformative power of the present, and stepping confidently into a future filled with limitless possibilities.

This transition requires us to cultivate a sense of self-awareness, to challenge our limiting beliefs, and to redefine our relationship with the past. It's about recognizing the power of our own narratives, the stories we tell ourselves about who we are and what we're capable of.

Here are some practical steps that can help us shift towards a growth mindset:

Challenge Your Limiting Beliefs: Start by identifying the beliefs that hold you back. Ask yourself questions like, "What beliefs am I holding onto that are preventing me from moving forward?" "What stories am I telling myself about my abilities?" Once you've identified these limiting beliefs, start to challenge them. Ask yourself, "Is this belief truly accurate?" "Is there evidence to support it?"

Embrace Failure as a Learning Opportunity: We all make mistakes, and failure is an inevitable part of life. Instead of viewing failures as setbacks, see them as opportunities to learn, grow, and adapt. Analyze your mistakes, identify the lessons they hold, and use that knowledge to move forward.

Focus on Your Strengths: We all have unique talents, skills, and strengths. Focus on what you do well and how you can leverage those strengths to achieve your goals. Remember, you don't have to be good at everything – focus on developing and nurturing the abilities that you excel in.

Seek Out Challenges: Stepping outside of your comfort zone is essential for growth. Challenge yourself to try new things, take on new responsibilities, and push your boundaries. The more you challenge yourself, the more you will learn and the more resilient you will become.

Practice Gratitude: Gratitude is a powerful tool for shifting your mindset. Take time to appreciate the positive aspects of your life, both big and small. Focusing on gratitude can help you to cultivate a more optimistic outlook, appreciate the present moment, and embrace the journey of growth.

Visualize Your Success: Visualization is a powerful technique that can help you to achieve your goals. Imagine yourself achieving your dreams, experiencing success, and overcoming obstacles. This visualization process can help you to develop a more positive outlook and strengthen your belief in your own abilities.

Surround Yourself with Positive Influences: The people we surround ourselves with have a significant impact on our mindset. Seek out friends, mentors, and role models who inspire you, challenge you, and support your growth. Surround yourself with people who believe in you and encourage you to achieve your full potential.

Embracing a growth mindset is not a one-time event, but rather, a continuous process. It requires conscious effort, persistence, and a willingness to challenge our limiting beliefs and embrace the transformative power of change. As we cultivate a growth mindset, we open ourselves to new possibilities, unleash our potential, and embrace the journey of personal growth and transformation.

Just as Purvi embarked on her journey abroad, we too can step confidently into the unknown, fueled by a growth mindset, and empowered to create a life filled with purpose, fulfillment, and endless opportunities. Let us learn to embrace the present, rewrite our narratives, and rewrite our stories, embracing the challenges and opportunities that come our way, for in these challenges lies our greatest growth.

<u>Stories of Renewal</u>

The stories of renewal are a testament to the human spirit's resilience and ability to thrive even after facing life's most daunting challenges. These tales offer a beacon of hope, reminding us that new beginnings are always possible, regardless of the storms we have weathered.

One such story is that of **Shree**, a young woman who found herself at a crossroads in her life. After years of pursuing a career in finance, Shree realized that it was not fulfilling her. She felt trapped in a cycle of long hours, constant pressure, and a sense of detachment from her true passions. The weight of societal expectations, the fear of failure, and the comfort of familiarity held her captive. But deep inside, a yearning for something more, something authentically hers, was growing stronger with each passing day.

Shree's story is not unique. It resonates with many of us who have found ourselves tethered to paths that no longer serve us, paths we have chosen for various reasons, sometimes out of obligation, fear, or even a sense of duty. But Shree's story also highlights the courage it takes to break free, to listen to that inner voice that whispers of a different life, a life that aligns with our true selves.

After much introspection and soul-searching, Shree decided to make a bold move. She left her secure job, despite the apprehensions of her family and friends, to pursue her passion for pottery. It was a leap of faith, a step into the unknown, filled with both excitement and uncertainty. Her journey was not without its challenges. Financial insecurity, the need to build a new network, and the fear of failure all loomed. But Shree was determined. She enrolled in pottery classes, attended workshops, and even started a small pottery studio in her home.

Slowly but surely, Shree's new path began to take shape. Her pottery became a form of self-expression, her hands shaping clay into beautiful pieces that reflected her journey of rediscovery. She found a sense of purpose and fulfillment she had never experienced before. Her work resonated with others, and she began to sell her pieces at local craft fairs and galleries.

Shree's story serves as a powerful reminder that it is never too late to embark on a new beginning, to embrace change, and to rewrite our narratives. Her transformation demonstrates the power of aligning our actions with our passions.

Another inspiring story is that of **Ram**, a retired teacher who had spent his life dedicated to educating young minds. Raj's life had been filled with meaning and purpose, but after retirement, he found himself adrift, lacking a sense of direction. The routines and rituals of his previous life had disappeared, leaving a void that he struggled to fill.

Ram's story speaks to the common experience of individuals who have dedicated years to a particular path, and who find themselves facing a new chapter after a significant life transition. The transition from a structured routine to a less defined period can be challenging, as it often requires us to rediscover our purpose and create new meaning in our lives.

Ram's journey of renewal began with a simple act of curiosity. He had always been fascinated by the art of storytelling and had a keen interest in ancient Indian epics. He decided to explore these stories in depth, not just as a reader, but as a storyteller. He joined a local storytelling group, where he shared his knowledge and passion for Indian folklore.

His journey took him to ancient temples and forgotten villages, where he collected oral traditions and myths from local elders. Ram's storytelling became a way for him to connect with the wisdom of his ancestors, to bridge the gap between the past and the present. He realized that his passion for storytelling could become a platform for cultural preservation and community engagement.

Ram's story underlines the transformative power of pursuing our passions, even in the later stages of life. It teaches us that a new chapter can be filled with purpose and meaning, even if it takes us to unexpected and uncharted territories. It emphasizes that life is a continuous journey of growth and evolution, and that we can find fulfillment at every stage.

The stories of Shree and Ram, along with countless others who have embraced new beginnings, remind us that change is an inherent part of life.

It is not something to be feared but rather embraced as an opportunity for growth, renewal, and self-discovery. New beginnings can emerge from adversity, from the realization that our current paths are not serving us, or simply from the natural ebb and flow of life.

Whether we are making a radical shift in our careers, navigating personal transitions, or simply seeking a deeper sense of fulfillment, the stories of renewal offer a powerful message: We have the power to choose a new path, to create a future that aligns with our values and aspirations, and to live a life that is both meaningful and fulfilling. These stories are a testament to the resilience of the human spirit, a reminder that new beginnings are always within our reach, and a source of inspiration for us to embark on our own journeys of renewal.

Creating your New Path

Embracing new beginnings often feels like stepping onto unfamiliar terrain, a journey into the unknown. The fear of the unknown, that nagging voice whispering doubts and anxieties, can be a formidable opponent. Yet, within that fear lies a potent opportunity for growth and transformation. It's the chance to break free from the patterns of the past, to shed the limitations that have held us back, and to step into a future brimming with possibilities.

To navigate this path, we must cultivate a "growth mindset," a mental framework that embraces challenges as opportunities for learning and development. This shift in perspective allows us to view setbacks not as failures, but as stepping stones on the road to success. It's about recognizing that change isn't something to fear, but rather a natural and essential part of life's grand tapestry.

Taking the first step can feel daunting, but it's the most crucial step. The act of making a decision, of committing to a new path, is a powerful affirmation of our own agency. It's a testament to our ability to take control of our destinies. Think of it as a seed, planted in fertile ground, waiting to sprout and grow.

To make that first step a bit easier, consider the following strategies:

1. Define Your Vision: Imagine your ideal future, a vision of your life free from the constraints of the past. What does it look like? What are you doing? Who are you with? By envisioning your desired future, you provide yourself with a compass and a guiding light.

2. Set Small, Achievable Goals: The journey to a new beginning rarely happens overnight. It's a gradual process, a series of small steps that lead to significant change. Break down your larger vision into smaller, manageable goals, each one a milestone on the path. Celebrate each achievement, no matter how small, to keep the momentum going.

3. Embrace Imperfection: It's okay to stumble, to make mistakes, to take a wrong turn. Remember, the journey is just as important as the destination. Each misstep is an opportunity to learn, to adjust your course, and to grow stronger. Embrace the imperfections, for they are the essence of human experience.

4. Seek Support and Guidance: You don't have to navigate this journey alone. Reach out to trusted friends, family members, mentors, or even a therapist. Sharing your hopes, fears, and aspirations with others can provide valuable support and encouragement.

5. Practice Self-Compassion: Be gentle with yourself as you embark on this journey. Acknowledge the emotions that arise, the fear, the uncertainty, the self-doubt. Embrace them as part of the process, and treat yourself with the same kindness you would offer a dear friend.

Stories of Renewal

To illustrate the transformative power of embracing new beginnings, let's delve into some inspiring stories from Indian culture:

The Story of the Phoenix: In ancient Indian mythology, the phoenix, a majestic bird, is known for its ability to rise from ashes. When its life comes to an end, it consumes itself in fire, only to be reborn from the flames, stronger and more vibrant than before. This cyclical rebirth is a powerful symbol of renewal, of the ability to overcome adversity and emerge transformed.

The Tale of the Warrior Princess: The epic story of the Mahabharata features a valiant warrior princess, Draupadi, who defied societal norms and faced numerous challenges with courage and grace. Her story highlights the resilience of the human spirit, its ability to overcome adversity and emerge victorious. Draupadi's unwavering spirit serves as an inspiration to anyone seeking to break free from the shackles of the past and embrace a brighter future.

The Path of the Pilgrim: In Hinduism, the concept of pilgrimage plays a significant role in personal and spiritual growth. Pilgrims embark on journeys, often long and arduous, to seek enlightenment and a deeper connection with the divine. The journey itself is a transformative experience, a process of self-discovery and spiritual awakening. Pilgrims learn to overcome obstacles, to cultivate resilience, and to embrace the challenges of life with a renewed sense of purpose.

Creating Your New Path

Embracing a new beginning is about more than just starting anew; it's about actively creating the life you desire. It's about forging a path that aligns with your values, dreams, and aspirations. This creation process begins with a commitment to self-awareness, to understanding your strengths, weaknesses, and desires.

1. Reflect on Your Values: What are the core principles that guide your life? What matters most to you? By understanding your values, you can identify the direction you want your life to take.

2. Explore Your Passions: What brings you joy and fulfillment? What makes your heart sing? Don't be afraid to step outside your comfort zone and explore new possibilities.

3. Identify Your Skills and Talents: What are you good at? What natural abilities do you possess? These skills can be your tools, your assets, your stepping stones on the path to success.

4. Embrace Learning and Growth: The journey of self-improvement is never-ending. Be open to learning new skills, expanding your knowledge, and challenging yourself to grow.

5. Seek Mentorship and Guidance: Connecting with experienced mentors or coaches can provide invaluable support and guidance as you create your new path. They can offer insights, challenge your thinking, and help you stay focused on your goals.

6. Embrace Imperfection: As you navigate this creative process, remember that imperfection is a part of the journey. Allow yourself to experiment, to make mistakes, and to learn from them.

7. Trust Your Intuition: Listen to that inner voice, your gut feeling. It can provide valuable insights and guide you towards the right choices.

8. Embrace the Power of Now: Don't get lost in the "what ifs" and the "should haves" of the past. Focus on the present moment, the here and now. This is where your power lies, where you have the ability to shape your future.

Embracing a new beginning is not a passive act; it's an active choice. It's a decision to break free from the limitations of the past and to step into a future filled with possibilities. It's about trusting yourself, embracing your strengths, and believing that you have the power to create the life you desire. It's about recognizing that within each of us lies the potential for transformation, the ability to rise from the ashes, like the phoenix, and create a new, vibrant, and fulfilling future.

10

LIVING FULLY IN THE PRESENT

The Essence of Presence

The essence of presence is the ability to be fully engaged in the here and now, without dwelling on the past or worrying about the future. It's about experiencing the richness of each moment, savoring the flavors of your cup of chai, noticing the gentle caress of the breeze on your skin, or simply being present in a conversation with a loved one.

Living in the present is not about ignoring the past or denying its influence; it's about recognizing its lessons and letting go of its grip. It's about acknowledging that the past has shaped you, but it doesn't define you. It's about realizing that you have the power to choose your present moment, and in doing so, you choose your future.

Imagine a busy street in Mumbai, a symphony of sights, sounds, and smells. The honking of cars, the chatter of street vendors, the aroma of spices wafting from nearby restaurants – all these elements contribute to the vibrant tapestry of the present moment. But if you're lost in your thoughts about a missed opportunity, a past argument, or a future deadline, you're missing out on the richness of this bustling scene. You're not truly experiencing the vibrant life unfolding around you.

The same principle applies to our daily lives. When we're consumed by anxieties about the future or regrets about the past, we miss the beauty and joy that exists in the present moment. We disconnect from the simple pleasures of a sunrise, the warmth of a hug, the laughter shared with friends.

The truth is, the present moment is all we truly have. The past is gone, and the future is yet to come. We can't change what has already happened, and we can't control what will happen tomorrow. But we can choose how we experience the present moment.

The first step towards living fully in the present is becoming aware of our thoughts and feelings. Notice the constant chatter in your mind, the anxieties that swirl around you, the regrets that cling to your past. Don't judge these thoughts or feelings; simply observe them without judgment. Like the bustling street in Mumbai, they are part of the vibrant tapestry of your experience.

Once you've become aware of your thoughts, you can begin to shift your attention to the present moment. Focus on your senses – the sights, sounds, smells, tastes, and textures around you. Feel the ground beneath your feet, the warmth of the sun on your skin, the gentle breeze on your face. Engage in activities that bring you joy, such as listening to music, spending time in nature, or engaging in a creative pursuit.

Living in the present is not a passive act; it requires conscious effort. It's like training a muscle; the more you practice, the stronger it becomes. You may find yourself slipping back into your thoughts from time to time, but that's okay. Simply acknowledge the thought, gently let it go, and return your attention to the present moment.

<u>There are many techniques that can help you enhance your presence, including:</u>

Mindfulness Meditation: This practice involves focusing your attention on your breath, sensations in your body, or a chosen object. By bringing your awareness to the present moment, you can learn to observe your thoughts and feelings without judgment.

Yoga: This ancient practice combines physical postures, breathing techniques, and meditation. Yoga helps to calm the mind, improve focus, and cultivate a sense of inner peace.

Gratitude Journaling: Taking a few minutes each day to write down what you are grateful for can help to shift your focus to the positive aspects of your life.

Mindful Walking: Paying attention to your footsteps, the sensations of your body, and the environment around you can transform a simple walk into a mindful practice.

Engaging in Meaningful Activities: Finding activities that bring you joy and purpose can help you to feel more present and engaged in life.

Cultivating presence not only enhances your personal experience but also strengthens your relationships. When you're present with someone, you're giving them your full attention, showing them that they are important and valued. You're actively listening, engaging in the conversation, and creating a genuine connection.

Imagine the impact of being fully present in your conversations with friends and family. Instead of being distracted by your phone or lost in your thoughts, you are actively listening, engaging in their stories, and offering your support. You're creating a space for connection, understanding, and love.

Living fully in the present is a gift you give yourself and those around you. It's a journey of self-discovery, a path to inner peace, and a gateway to a more fulfilling life. It's about embracing the beauty of each moment, savoring the sweetness of life, and appreciating the gift of now.

As you journey towards presence, you may encounter resistance. Your mind may try to pull you back into the past or worry about the future. But with each conscious act of bringing your attention to the present moment, you weaken the grip of those distractions. You learn to embrace the flow of life, accepting the ups and downs, the joys and sorrows, with grace and resilience.

The journey towards presence is not a destination, but a continuous practice. It's about becoming more aware of each moment, appreciating the beauty of the now, and choosing to live your life to the fullest, one moment at a time. Embrace the present moment, and you'll discover a world of possibilities, a life filled with purpose, joy, and deep connection.

The stories of individuals who have transformed their lives by living in the present are a testament to the transformative power of presence. They have learned to let go of the past, embrace the present, and create a future filled with meaning and purpose. Their journeys are an inspiration, a reminder that a life lived fully in the present is a life truly lived.

Practices to Enhance Presence

The concept of presence might seem simple, a fleeting notion we often grasp at in moments of quiet reflection or deep connection. But truly inhabiting the present moment, letting go of the past and the anxieties of the future, is an art form. It's a practice, a conscious choice we make every day to experience life with heightened awareness and intention.

Imagine a vibrant tapestry woven with threads of color, each representing a moment in your life. There are threads of joy and sorrow, of triumph and failure, of love and loss. The past is woven into this tapestry, but dwelling on it, either in its glory or its shadows, can pull us away from the beauty of the present. We become entangled in the threads of yesterday, unable to fully appreciate the richness and texture of the present moment.

To live fully in the present is to embrace the now. It's about tuning in to the symphony of life – the rustling leaves outside your window, the warmth of the sun on your skin, the taste of your morning tea. It's about being fully present in conversations, in experiences, in the simple act of breathing. It's about recognizing that each moment, no matter how mundane, holds the potential for beauty, connection, and meaning.

Techniques to Enhance Presence

Mindfulness: The Foundation of Presence

Mindfulness is the cornerstone of living in the present moment. It's the practice of paying attention to the present experience without judgment. It's about observing our thoughts, emotions, and sensations with a gentle, non-reactive awareness. Mindfulness is not about emptying our minds, but rather about becoming aware of what arises within us and around us, without getting caught up in the stories we tell ourselves about these experiences.

Think of mindfulness as a lighthouse guiding you through the stormy seas of your thoughts and emotions. You might be caught in the currents of worry about the future or the undertow of past regrets, but mindfulness helps you to stay grounded in the present moment, allowing you to see the horizon clearly and navigate towards calmer waters.

<u>How to cultivate mindfulness:</u>

Mindful Breathing: One of the simplest yet most powerful ways to cultivate mindfulness is through conscious breathing. Sit comfortably, close your eyes, and focus your attention on the natural rise and fall of your breath. Notice the sensation of air entering and leaving your nostrils, the subtle expansion and contraction of your chest. If your mind wanders, gently bring it back to your breath.

Body Scan Meditation: Another effective technique is the body scan. Lie down comfortably or sit in a chair with your spine straight. Bring your awareness to your body, starting with your toes. Gently scan your body, noticing any sensations – warmth, tingling, pressure, or tightness. Move slowly from your toes to your feet, your legs, your torso, your arms, and finally to your head, paying attention to each part of your body.

Mindful Walking: Even walking can be a form of mindfulness. As you walk, focus your attention on the sensation of your feet on the ground, the rhythm of your steps, the movement of your arms. Notice the sounds around you – birds chirping, traffic noise, the wind in the trees. Engage all your senses in the experience of walking.

Mindful Eating: Turn mealtimes into a mindful practice. Before you eat, take a moment to appreciate the food. Observe its colors, its textures, its aroma. As you eat, savor each bite. Notice the flavors and the sensations in your mouth. Eat slowly and mindfully, appreciating the experience of nourishing your body.

The Power of Gratitude

Gratitude is another powerful tool for cultivating presence. When we focus on what we are grateful for, we shift our attention from what we lack to what we have. We become more aware of the good things in our lives, the simple joys and blessings that often go unnoticed.

Imagine a garden filled with vibrant flowers. When we focus on the weeds, the thorns, and the imperfections, we miss the beauty of the blooms. But when we turn our attention to the vibrant colors, the delicate petals, and the sweet fragrance, we experience the garden in its fullness. Gratitude is like that – it helps us see the beauty and abundance in our lives, even amidst challenges.

How to cultivate gratitude:

Gratitude Journal: Write down things you are grateful for each day. This could be anything from a beautiful sunrise to a kind gesture from a stranger to the love of your family. Reflecting on these things regularly helps shift your focus to the positive.

Gratitude List: Create a list of things you are grateful for, ranging from the simple to the profound. Review this list whenever you feel overwhelmed or stressed to remind yourself of all the good things in your life.

Gratitude Rituals: Incorporate gratitude into your daily routine. Before bed, take a few minutes to reflect on the good things that happened that day. Or, start your morning with a gratitude meditation, focusing on what you are thankful for.

The Art of Active Listening

Active listening is not just about hearing words, but about truly understanding the speaker's perspective. It involves paying attention to both verbal and non-verbal cues, showing genuine interest in what the other person is saying, and responding in a way that demonstrates understanding and empathy.

Think of active listening as a bridge connecting two people. When we listen actively, we build a bridge of understanding and connection, allowing us to connect with another person on a deeper level.

<u>How to practice active listening:</u>

Make eye contact: Focus your attention on the speaker and make eye contact. This shows that you are engaged and present in the conversation.

Listen with your whole body: Lean in slightly, nod your head, and use facial expressions to indicate that you are listening and understanding.

Ask clarifying questions: If you don't understand something, ask questions to clarify the speaker's meaning.

Summarize and reflect: After the speaker has finished, summarize what you have heard to make sure you have understood their perspective.

Avoid interrupting: Let the speaker finish their thoughts before offering your own input.

The Power of Being Present in Relationships

Being present in our relationships is crucial for fostering connection and intimacy. It's about putting down our phones, turning off the TV, and giving our full attention to the people we love. It's about listening to their joys and sorrows, celebrating their successes, and offering support during their challenges.

Imagine a campfire with friends and loved ones gathered around. When we are present in the moment, we are fully engaged in the warmth of the fire, the laughter and stories shared, the deep connection that comes from being truly present with each other.

<u>How to enhance presence in relationships:</u>

Quality time over quantity: Spend meaningful time with loved ones, even if it's just a few minutes, rather than rushed moments filled with distractions.

Put away the distractions: Turn off your phone, close your laptop, and put away anything that might distract you from being fully present with the person you are with.

Show genuine interest: Ask questions, listen attentively, and make eye contact. Show that you are truly interested in what the other person has to say.

Embrace the small moments: Find joy in the simple things, like a shared meal, a walk in the park, or just sitting quietly together.

Express appreciation: Let loved ones know how much you care about them and appreciate their presence in your life.

Living Your Best Life Now

Living fully in the present is not about escaping from reality or ignoring challenges. It's about embracing life in its entirety – the joy and the sorrow, the successes and the setbacks. It's about recognizing that every moment is a gift, an opportunity to learn, grow, and connect with the world around us.

Think of life as a river flowing towards the sea. The current might be strong, there might be rapids and waterfalls, but the journey itself is beautiful and meaningful. Living in the present is about fully experiencing each moment of the flow, not clinging to the past or fearing the future, but simply being present in the now.

How to embrace the present moment:

Appreciate the simple things: Find joy in the little things – the taste of your coffee, the warmth of the sun, the laughter of a child.

Focus on the moment: When your mind wanders, gently bring it back to the present moment. What are you seeing, hearing, feeling, smelling, tasting?

Engage your senses: Pay attention to your senses and immerse yourself in the present experience.

Practice gratitude: Take time each day to reflect on what you are grateful for.

Be present in conversations: Listen actively, show genuine interest, and be fully engaged in the conversation.

Embrace change: Change is inevitable, but we can choose to meet it with openness and curiosity.

Practice forgiveness: Let go of past hurts and resentments to free yourself from the burdens of the past.

Seek joy in the journey: Focus on the present moment and appreciate the journey, not just the destination.

Living fully in the present is a continuous practice, a journey of self-discovery and transformation. It's about letting go of the past, embracing the present, and stepping into the future with a sense of intention, joy, and gratitude.

As you embark on this journey, remember that you are not alone. There is a deep well of wisdom and support within you and around you. Embrace the challenges, celebrate the triumphs, and live each moment to the fullest. You are worthy of a life filled with presence, joy, and purpose.

<u>The Impact of Presence on Relationships</u>

Imagine a bustling marketplace in India, filled with vibrant colors, enticing aromas, and the constant hum of conversations. In the midst of this vibrant scene, a vendor diligently attends to his stall, his eyes alert, his hands deftly arranging his wares. He is fully present, engaged in the moment, his attention focused on each customer who approaches. This, in essence, is the power of presence – the ability to be fully engaged with the here and now, to savor the richness of each moment, and to connect deeply with those around us.

Presence isn't merely about being physically in a particular place; it's a state of mind, a conscious choice to relinquish the grip of the past and the anxieties of the future, and to fully embrace the present moment. When we cultivate presence, we unlock a profound transformation in our lives, particularly in our relationships. Our connections with others deepen, our communication becomes more authentic, and our ability to build meaningful bonds strengthens.

Imagine a couple sitting together, sharing a meal. One partner, consumed by thoughts about work deadlines or past disagreements, barely notices the flavors of the food or the warmth in the other's gaze. The other, however, is fully present, savoring every bite, genuinely listening to their partner's stories, and responding with heartfelt connection. This stark contrast highlights the impact of presence on relationships. When we are present, we create a space for genuine intimacy, for understanding, and for shared experiences that nourish our bonds.

Think of the power of a simple gesture, a loving touch, a heartfelt compliment, when offered with full presence. The impact is amplified tenfold, creating a ripple effect of warmth and connection. Our presence isn't just about ourselves; it's a gift we offer to those we care about, a way to show them that we are truly present in their lives, attentive to their needs, and invested in their well-being.

In a world that constantly demands our attention, it's easy to become distracted, to let our minds wander to past regrets or future worries. This constant mental chatter can create a barrier between us and those we love, hindering our ability to connect deeply and meaningfully. The practice of presence, however, provides a powerful antidote to this disconnection. It's a reminder that the most fulfilling relationships are built on the foundation of shared moments, of genuine listening, of being fully present in the here and now.

Think of a family gathered for a celebration. The table is laden with food, laughter fills the air, and children's excited chatter intertwines with the stories of elders. Yet, amidst this joyous scene, some may be caught in the grip of their phones, scrolling through social media, their minds elsewhere. Others, however, are fully present, their eyes sparkling with laughter, their hearts engaged in the shared experience. This is the magic of presence, the ability to be fully immersed in the joy of the moment, to create lasting memories that bind us together.

This is not to say that being present is a constant state of bliss, free from any challenges. Life, with its inherent complexities, throws unexpected curveballs our way. We may encounter disagreements, experience moments of frustration, or face difficult conversations. It's in these moments, however, that the power of presence becomes truly evident. When we approach these challenges with presence, we are less likely to react impulsively, to let past grievances cloud our judgment, or to allow fear to dictate our responses. Instead, we can engage with a sense of calm, clarity, and empathy, allowing us to navigate these difficult waters with greater understanding and grace.

Imagine a couple engaged in a heated argument. One partner, fueled by past resentments and a desire to win, throws hurtful words like daggers, further fueling the flames of conflict. The other, however, drawing on the power of presence, takes a deep breath, acknowledges their partner's pain, and chooses to respond with compassion rather than retaliation. This is the transformative power of presence in conflict – the ability to remain grounded in the present moment, to see through the fog of emotions, and to choose a path of understanding and resolution.

In our fast-paced world, it's tempting to constantly chase the next big thing, to seek fulfillment in external achievements, and to ignore the simple joys of the present moment. But it is in the quiet moments, in the genuine connections, in the mindful appreciation of the ordinary, that we find true meaning and lasting happiness. Cultivating presence is not just a self-improvement strategy; it's a transformative journey that unlocks the door to deeper connections, more fulfilling relationships, and a richer, more meaningful life.

<u>Here are some practical ways to cultivate presence in your relationships:</u>

Make eye contact: When engaging in conversation, consciously make eye contact with your partner, showing them that you are truly listening and attentive.

Put away distractions: Minimize distractions, like phones, television, or other screens, to create a space where you can give your undivided attention.

Practice active listening: Focus on what your partner is saying, both verbally and nonverbally. Reflect back on their words to demonstrate understanding and empathy.

Show appreciation: Express gratitude for the small things, the gestures of kindness, the shared moments that enrich your connection.

Engage in mindful activities together: Find activities that allow you to be present together, such as taking a walk in nature, cooking a meal, or simply enjoying a cup of tea in silence.

Embrace the power of touch: A gentle touch, a warm hug, a loving hand on a shoulder can convey more than words can express.

Practice forgiveness: Let go of past hurts and grudges, allowing you to move forward in your relationship with a clear heart and an open mind.

These are just a few starting points. As you cultivate presence in your relationships, you will discover your own unique ways to connect more deeply, to savor the precious moments, and to build a foundation of trust and understanding that will last a lifetime. Remember, presence is not a destination, but a journey, a conscious choice to be fully engaged in the unfolding of life, in the company of those you cherish. It's a choice that can transform your relationships, enriching them with meaning, depth, and a profound sense of connection.

Living your Best Life Now

The sun dips below the horizon, painting the sky with hues of orange and violet, casting long shadows that stretch across the bustling streets of Mumbai. As the city slowly winds down, a sense of peace descends upon the air. It's a moment of quiet reflection, a reminder that life, in its relentless rush, often forgets to pause. This is the essence of presence – the ability to truly be in the moment, to savor the symphony of senses that surround us, to be fully present, not just physically but mentally and emotionally.

Imagine a small tea stall nestled in a quiet corner of a bustling market in Delhi. The aroma of freshly brewed chai fills the air, mingling with the scent of spices and the chatter of vendors. A young man sits at the stall, sipping his chai, his eyes closed, his mind calm. He doesn't think about the past, nor does he worry about the future. He is simply present, embracing the warmth of the chai, the symphony of sounds, the vibrant chaos of life unfolding around him. This is the power of living in the present – a state of being that allows us to truly appreciate the richness of each moment.

But living in the present is more than just a fleeting state of being. It's a conscious choice, a practice that requires effort, patience, and a willingness to let go of the past and the future. It's about shedding the weight of yesterday's burdens and anxieties about tomorrow's uncertainties, and embracing the beauty of the here and now.

For those steeped in Indian culture, this concept of living in the present finds resonance in the ancient wisdom of mindfulness, which emphasizes the importance of being fully aware of the present moment. This awareness, cultivated through practices like meditation, helps us to quiet the incessant chatter of our minds, allowing us to experience the world with renewed clarity and appreciation.

To embrace this mindful approach to life, it's crucial to recognize the subtle ways our minds constantly drift away from the present moment. We might find ourselves lost in thoughts about past regrets, anxieties about future challenges, or simply daydreaming about what we'd rather be doing. These mental excursions, while seemingly harmless, rob us of the richness of the present.

<u>Here are some practical ways to cultivate presence and live life to the fullest:</u>

1. The Power of Observation:

Cultivate the habit of observing the world around you with renewed attention. When you walk down the street, notice the colors, the sounds, the textures, and the movements of people. When you eat a meal, pay attention to the taste, the aroma, and the texture of the food. This mindful observation helps shift your focus from the constant stream of thoughts to the immediate experience.

2. The Gift of Mindfulness:

Incorporate mindfulness practices into your daily routine. This could include meditation, where you focus on your breath and observe your thoughts without judgment, or simply taking a few moments each day to sit quietly and notice the sensations in your body. Mindfulness helps you become more aware of your thoughts and feelings, allowing you to detach from them and regain control of your mind.

3. The Art of Gratitude:

Gratitude is a powerful tool for living in the present moment. When you practice gratitude, you focus on the good things in your life, appreciating the blessings you often take for granted. This simple act of acknowledging the positive aspects of your life shifts your perspective, making you more aware of the good things that are happening around you.

4. The Importance of Connection:

Our relationships are a vital part of our present moment. When we engage in meaningful conversations, listen attentively to others, and share experiences with those we care about, we create a sense of connection that grounds us in the present. These interactions enrich our lives and remind us that we are not alone in our journey.

5. The Magic of Simple Pleasures:

Often, the greatest joys lie in the simplest of things. A cup of tea on a rainy day, a walk in nature, a heartfelt conversation with a loved one – these seemingly ordinary moments, when fully embraced, can become extraordinary. By finding joy in the everyday, we cultivate a sense of contentment and gratitude that deepens our connection to the present moment.

6. The Power of Letting Go:

One of the key ingredients to living in the present is learning to let go. This doesn't mean giving up on your dreams or ignoring your responsibilities. It means releasing the attachments to past regrets, fears, and worries that weigh you down. This can be a challenging process, but it is essential for freeing your mind and allowing you to fully engage in the present.

7. The Beauty of Acceptance:

Life is a constant flow of change, and resisting this inevitable flow is a sure recipe for unhappiness. Learning to accept what is, even when it is difficult or unpleasant, is a key to living in the present. Acceptance allows you to move through challenges with more grace and resilience, without getting bogged down in resistance or denial.

8. The Importance of Self-Care:

Self-care is not a luxury; it's a necessity for living a fulfilling life. When you prioritize self-care, you create space for reflection, relaxation, and renewal.

Whether it's through yoga, meditation, spending time in nature, or simply indulging in a hobby you enjoy, taking care of yourself allows you to recharge your mind and body, enhancing your ability to be fully present.

9. The Power of Forgiveness:

Holding onto anger, resentment, or guilt from the past can cloud your mind and prevent you from fully experiencing the present. Forgiveness, while challenging, is a powerful tool for letting go of the past and embracing the present. When you forgive yourself and others, you free yourself from the emotional weight of the past, creating space for joy, peace, and healing.

10. The Art of Intention:

Start each day with intention, setting a clear purpose for your actions. This could be as simple as making a conscious choice to be present in your interactions, to focus on the positive aspects of your life, or to engage in activities that bring you joy. By setting intentions, you create a roadmap for navigating your day with mindfulness and purpose.

11. The Value of Rituals:

Incorporating rituals into your daily routine can enhance your connection to the present moment. These rituals can be simple, like taking a few minutes to appreciate the beauty of a sunrise or sunset, enjoying a cup of tea with intention, or spending time in nature. By creating these mindful moments, you cultivate a sense of presence and gratitude that enriches your daily experience.

The journey of living in the present is an ongoing one, a constant practice of cultivating awareness, letting go of the past, and embracing the richness of each moment. It's a journey that requires patience, perseverance, and a willingness to embrace the transformative power of presence.

As you navigate the complexities of life, remember the wisdom of the ancient Indian proverb, "The best time to plant a tree was twenty years ago. The second best time is today." Embrace the present, for it is the only moment you truly have control over. It's the moment that holds the potential for joy, growth, and fulfillment. Live it fully, with intention and gratitude, and you'll discover the magic of living your best life now.

Stories of PresentMinded Living

The power of living fully in the present moment is a concept deeply ingrained in many Eastern philosophies, particularly in Indian culture. It is about shedding the burdens of the past and the anxieties of the future to experience the richness of the now. While this may seem simple in theory, it is a practice that requires conscious effort and dedication.

Imagine a young woman named **Reva**, who lived a life shrouded by the shadows of her past. A tumultuous childhood filled with parental discord and financial struggles had left her with a deep sense of insecurity and a constant fear of failure. This fear translated into a constant replay of past mistakes, a relentless internal critic that drowned out any possibility of joy in the present. Her days were spent consumed by anxiety, unable to fully engage in the joys and opportunities that life presented.

Then, a chance encounter with an elderly wisdom teacher at a meditation retreat sparked a shift within Reva. This teacher, a kind and gentle soul, spoke of the transformative power of the present moment, of how letting go of the past could unlock a world of peace and fulfillment. He shared stories of individuals who had risen above their own personal tragedies, finding solace and joy in embracing the present.

Reva decided to embark on this path of self-discovery. She began practicing mindfulness, learning to observe her thoughts and emotions without judgment. She started to notice the constant stream of negative thoughts, the replay of past hurts, and the anxieties about the future. Through conscious effort, she began to gently redirect her attention to the present moment, focusing on the sensations of her breath, the sounds around her, and the warmth of the sun on her skin.

Initially, it was a struggle. The past had a strong grip on her, a relentless voice that whispered doubts and fears. But with each practice session, Reva became more adept at recognizing these negative patterns and gently redirecting her attention back to the present.

Gradually, her life began to transform. The weight of the past began to lift, replaced by a newfound sense of peace and clarity. She found herself more present in conversations, more attentive to the needs of those around her. She started to see the world with fresh eyes, appreciating the beauty in the mundane, the joy in the everyday.

As Reva embraced the present, she also started to experience a newfound sense of purpose. She was no longer defined by the past or burdened by the anxieties of the future. She was present, fully alive, and ready to create a future that was aligned with her authentic self.

Her journey wasn't without its challenges. There were moments of doubt, times when the past threatened to pull her back into its grip. However, she had discovered a new tool, a powerful anchor that brought her back to the present moment - mindfulness.

Reva's story is not unique. There are countless others who have transformed their lives by embracing the present. A young man named **Anil**, who had been haunted by the memories of a failed business venture, found solace in the present moment by dedicating himself to helping others. He volunteered at a local homeless shelter, where he found purpose and fulfillment in making a difference in the lives of those around him.

An elderly woman named **Shanti**, who had lost her husband after years of marriage, discovered a newfound joy in the present by reconnecting with her love for art. She enrolled in painting classes, rediscovering her passion and finding a new sense of purpose in her later years.

These are just a few examples of individuals who have discovered the transformative power of living fully in the present moment. It is a journey that requires courage, commitment, and a willingness to let go of the past. But for those who embark on this path, the rewards are immeasurable - a life filled with peace, purpose, and the joy of simply being.

ACKNOWLEDGEMENT

This book is the culmination of years of personal reflection, research, and conversations with countless individuals seeking to break free from the past. I am deeply grateful to all those who have shared their stories, insights, and experiences, shaping this journey of self-discovery.

My heartfelt gratitude goes to many individuals who provided support, inspiration, or feedback, whose unwavering belief in this project and insightful guidance have been instrumental in bringing it to fruition.

Thank you to my editor and co-author, my Husband, who has patiently guided me through the process, sharpening the message and ensuring clarity and impact.

To my family and friends, thank you for your constant support, encouragement, and love. Your belief in me has been my constant source of strength.

And finally, to all those who have chosen to embark on this journey of personal growth with me, thank you. Your presence and willingness to learn have made this endeavor truly meaningful.

GLOSSARY

Mindfulness:
A state of present moment awareness, achieved through focused attention without judgment.

Resilience:
The ability to adapt and bounce back from challenges and adversity.

Forgiveness:
The act of releasing resentment, anger, and blame toward oneself or others.

Gratitude:
An appreciation for the good things in one's life, fostering a positive outlook.

Present Moment:
The current experience, free from the constraints of past or future thoughts.

Cultural Norms:
Shared beliefs, values, and practices that define a particular culture or society.

Personal Narrative:
The story we tell ourselves about our life experiences, shaping our identity and perception.

REFERENCES

The book draws upon various sources to provide a comprehensive understanding of the themes explored. These references include:

Academic research and literature on human psychology, sociology, cultural studies, and self-help.

Personal accounts and stories shared by individuals who have embarked on their own journeys of growth and transformation.

Inspiring examples of social change and empowerment from diverse communities across India.

AUTHOR BIOGRAPHY

Anki Jain is an Indian writer seasoned with insightful observations on societal dynamics and human psychology. With a background and a

passion for storytelling, she weaves relatable narratives that resonate with Indian readers, exploring themes of cultural norms, personal growth, and the pursuit of a fulfilling life.

Her husband, co-author & editor, pen named **KOKO**, is a dedicated advocate for social change and believes in the power of individual transformation to create a more just and compassionate world. He has authored several articles exploring various aspects of human experience, including self-help, social commentary, and cultural analysis.

Their writing is characterized by a conversational and introspective tone, inviting readers to engage with their own inner journeys and to challenge the limitations they impose on themselves. Both of them are committed to fostering critical thinking, promoting empathy, and empowering individuals to live authentically and meaningfully.

Reach out to Authors: foranki@gmail.com | kokoforkp@gmail.com

BOOKS BY AUTHOR

<u>SERIES</u>

Unfortunately, how we Live

[LIFE] : living in the brackets

>PAST< : living in the yesters

"SELF" : living in the egotism

}LONE{ : living in the solitude

<u>INDIVIDUAL TITLES</u>

IKIGAI : finding your reason for being